Messiah

A Bible Study on the Lyrics of George Frideric Handel's *Messiah*

Paula Ann Brummel

Contents

To my father and mother, Pete and Nell Faber,
Thank you for creating such lasting memories
by taking me downtown Grand Rapids
to hear the Messiah!

To Peter and Abrielle,
Let's keep the tradition going!

Introduction

Handel's *Messiah* has been part of my life from my earliest years. The *Messiah* is an oratorio about the life of Christ. My father would put a large, flat, black disk into the record player, and out would come the composer's gorgeous music. Later, I listened to *Messiah* on tapes and CDs. Every December Dad took us down the wintry roads of Grand Rapids, Michigan, to hear the Calvin College Oratorio Society sing *Messiah*. Our family of five usually sat near the back of the hall. We often gazed through our binoculars for a better look at the musicians and soloists. God used these yearly performances to plant a love for the texts of *Messiah* in my heart. My husband and I now take our children to hear *Messiah* in Michigan City, Indiana. I love hearing my children walk around the house singing the familiar choruses.

During one of those performances at a Presbyterian church in Michigan City, Indiana, I noticed that while the oratorio continued, I wanted to linger and discover for myself how each text fit in the story of the Messiah. Afterward, I felt a desire to write a devotional that reflected on each passage. I hope you will turn over the passages with me in your mind and meditate on the life of Christ and His work in your behalf as you accompany me in this Bible study. The fifty-three lessons that follow are my thoughts on the beautiful biblical texts that Handel set to music.

George Frideric Handel was an eighteenth-century Baroque composer. He was born on February 23, 1685, in Germany. He received musical training in Halle-upon-Saale and later worked as a composer in Hamburg. He visited Italy before moving to London, where he made a name for himself. He arrived in London in 1712 and spent the rest of his life in the British Isles until he passed away at the age of seventy-four on April 14, 1759. He wrote many operas in the Italian style. His popularity with the British public fluctuated.

At age fifty-seven, Handel composed *Messiah* in an astonishingly short period of time: from August 22 to September 14,

1741. He was able to write this oratorio in twenty-four days because he could draw on musical ideas from his past. Also, the musical culture of his day demanded new operas to be created at a wild pace. He wrote *Messiah* using many flourishes and decorations in the music as he told the magnificent story of Christ. He set the words of the Bible to music, telling about Jesus's birth, death, resurrection, ascension, and second coming.

Handel did not come up with the lyrics or texts for *Messiah* himself. Charles Jennens, a friend of Handel, picked relevant Bible passages and placed them in a fitting order. Jennens selected Bible texts from the King James Bible and also used some King James Bible texts that were included in the Book of Common Prayer. Occasionally a word is inserted or replaced.

The new oratorio premiered in 1742 in Ireland. The first performance raised money for three charities, which included prisoner's debt relief, Mercer's Hospital, and a charitable infirmary. The oratorio was received with great excitement in Ireland.

Handel lived in the Age of Enlightenment when many Englishmen were rejecting the gospel. His oratorios were a powerful witness to the truth of the gospel. In his day, Pelagianism (the idea that man is basically good) and Deism (the idea that God is not active in the creation) were rampant. Many in England rejected basic Christian doctrines.

God used Handel's oratorio, *Messiah*, to broadcast the basic gospel message to many people. This oratorio should do more than entertain you; it should cause you to grow up in the knowledge of Christ. Although it was composed in a mere twenty-four days, its message has lasted hundreds of years.

Handel's mission is to tell the story of the Messiah in three segments:

I.   The prophesy and realization of God's plan to redeem mankind by the coming of the Messiah

II.   The accomplishment of redemption by the sacrifice of Jesus, mankind's rejection of God's offer, and mankind's utter defeat when trying to oppose the power of the Almighty

III. A hymn of thanksgiving for the final overthrow of death

Messiah 14 - Week Bible Study	*N̊.*
Week 1 **Part 1** **The Prophecy and Realization of God's Plan to Redeem Mankind by the Coming of the Messiah** ❖ the prophecy of salvation	N$^{os.}$ 1–4
Week 2 ❖ the prophecy of the coming of the Messiah and the question, despite (the prophecy of salvation), of what this may portend for the World	N$^{os.}$ 5–7
Week 3 ❖ the prophecy of the Virgin Birth	N$^{o.}$ 8-12
Week 4 ❖ the appearance of the Angels to the Shepherds	N$^{o.}$ 13-17

Week 5 ❖ Christ redemptive miracles on earth	N°. 18-21	

Week 6 **Part Two** *The Accomplishment of Redemption by the Sacrifice of Jesus, Man's Rejection of God's Offer, and Mankind's Utter Defeat When Trying to Oppose the Power of the Almighty* ❖ *the redemptive sacrifice, the scourging in the agony on the cross,*	N°. 22-26
Week 7 ❖ (Continued) the redemptive sacrifice, the scourging and the agony on the cross ❖ his sacrificial death, his passage through hell and resurrection	N°. 27-32
Week 8 ❖ his ascension ❖ God discloses his identity in Heaven	N°. 33-35
Week 9 ❖ Whitsun[1], the gift of tongues, the beginning of evangelism [1]"Whitsun" United Kingdom day of Pentecost	N°. 36-39

Week 10 ❖ the world and its rulers reject the gospel	Nᵒ· 40-42
Week 11 ❖ God's triumph	Nᵒ· 43-44
Week 12 **Part Three** *A Hymn of Thanksgiving for the Final Overthrow of Death* ❖ the promise of a bodily resurrection and redemption from Adam's fall	Nᵒ· 45-46
Week 13 ❖ the Day of Judgment and general Resurrection	Nᵒ· 47-48
Week 14 ❖ the victory over death and sin	No. 49-53

The titles, above, were found in the wordbook for the Messiah performed in 1743.

A Guide to the Original Source Texts for Handel's Messiah compiled by Martin P. Dicke

When using this Messiah Bible study, you will find it most helpful if you do the following:

1. Pray, asking God to reveal the Messiah to you in all His beauty.
2. Listen to and sing along with the part of *Messiah* you are studying.
3. Read the verses that speak about the Christ at the beginning of each lesson. Seven Old Testament books (Job, Psalms, Isaiah, Lamentations, Haggai, Zechariah, and Malachi) and seven New Testament books (Matthew, Luke, Romans, 1 Corinthians, Hebrews, 1 John, and Revelation) are referenced in *Messiah*.
4. Use this devotional to fuel and inspire further study about Jesus, the Messiah.

Most verses used in Handel's oratorio are from the Standard (Pure Cambridge) King James Version of the Bible. At times the text is quoted from the Book of Common Prayer (1662).

Messiah

Part 1

The Prophecy and Realization of God's Plan to Redeem Mankind by the Coming of the Messiah

Overture

The overture to *Messiah* sets the stage for the work that follows. Handel wove a distinct yet common thread throughout his entire work. Although the title of the work is *Messiah*, the word *messiah* never appears in the oratorio. Handel acquaints us with the Messiah's other beautiful names: Christ, Anointed, Lamb, Immanuel, Wonderful Counselor, King, Lord of Lords.

The title, *Messiah*, is succinct yet says so much. The Messiah is the one desired throughout the Old Testament. On opening my concordance to find the word messiah, I was shocked to find only four entries! The word *messiah* or *messias* is so familiar that I expected to see dozens of entries. The word occurs in two verses in the Old Testament book of Daniel and in two verses in the New Testament book of John. It is in John's Gospel that we discover the identity of the Messiah. In Daniel we read the following:

> Know therefore and understand, that from the going forth of the commandment to restore and to build Jerusalem unto the *Messiah* the Prince shall be seven weeks, and threescore and two weeks: the street shall be built again, and the wall, even in troublous times. (Daniel 9:25, emphasis added)

> And after threescore and two weeks shall *Messiah* be cut off, but not for himself: and the people of the prince that shall come shall destroy the city and the sanctuary; and the end thereof shall be with a flood, and unto the end of the war desolations are determined. (Daniel 9:26, emphasis added)

In the gospel of John we read:

> He first findeth his own brother Simon, and saith unto him, We have found the *Messias*, which is, being interpreted, the Christ. (John 1:41, emphasis added)
> The woman saith unto him, I know that *Messias* cometh, which is called Christ: when he is come, he will tell us all things. (John 4:25)
> From these verses we discover that the Messiah is Jesus Christ

and that He will tell us all things. The Old Testament, which was written in Hebrew, uses the word *messiah*, meaning "anointed one." The New Testament, which was written in Greek, uses Christ, which also means "anointed one." Christ is used as a title for Jesus; it points to His office as king and priest.

Several questions come to mind about the Anointed One:

- *What does it mean to be anointed?* To be anointed means that a person is equipped with the Holy Spirit to carry out a special office for which he has been chosen by God. Prophets, priests, and kings were anointed to their respective offices throughout the Old Testament.

- *When was Christ anointed?* Jesus Christ was anointed at His baptism in the Jordan River near Galilee (Matthew 3:13).

- *Who anointed Christ?* He was anointed by the Holy Spirit: "And Jesus, when he was baptized, went up straightway out of the water: and, lo, the heavens were opened unto him, and he saw the Spirit of God descending like a dove, and lighting upon him: and lo a voice from heaven, saying, This is my beloved Son, in whom I am well pleased" (Matthew 3:16–17).

- *How did Christ's anointing take place?* The anointing took place11). As the Spirit descended like a dove upon Him (Matthew 3:16).

- *What was Christ anointed to do?* He was anointed to be our prophet, priest, and king. God appointed Jesus to the office of Messiah, and this one office has a threefold dimension since Jesus is prophet, priest, and king. No person in the Old Testament served in all three offices. Isaiah was a prophet, but not a priest or king. Aaron was a priest, but not a prophet or king. Saul was a king, but not a priest. Melchizedek was a type of the Christ since he possessed both the offices of priest and king.

- How was Jesus an anointed a *prophet*? As our prophet, Christ teaches us the ways of God. He also instructs us about things that will come to pass. "And there came a fear on all: and they glorified God, saying, that a great prophet is risen up among us; and, that God hath visited his people" (Luke 7:16). "Then those men, when they had seen the miracle that Jesus did, said, this is of a truth that prophet that should come into the world" (John 6:14). "For Moses truly said unto the fathers, A prophet shall the Lord your God raise up unto you of your brethren, like unto me; him shall ye hear in all things whatsoever he shall say unto you" (Acts 3:22).

- How was Jesus anointed as a **priest**? As our high priest, Christ makes intercession with the Father on our behalf. He is the Mediator between God and man. By His death on the cross as a one-time sacrifice for the sins of His people, He paid for all the sins of His elect. "Wherefore in all things it behooved him to be made like unto his brethren, that he might be a merciful and faithful high priest in things pertaining to God, to make reconciliation for the sins of the people" (Hebrews 2:17). "Now of the things which we have spoken this is the sum: we have such a high priest, who is set on the right hand of the throne of the Majesty in the heavens" (Hebrews 8:1).

- How was Jesus anointed as a **king**? Christ was appointed to be the Lord and prince of His people. He is their powerful protector. He rules in the hearts of His people. He is a mighty warrior who will defeat all His enemies and ours. He reigns as the sovereign one over all things. All the inhabitants of the earth are His subjects. Behold, the days come, saith the Lord, that I will raise unto David a righteous Branch, and a king shall reign and prosper, and shall execute judgment and justice in the earth" (Jeremiah 23:5). "Nathaniel answered and saith unto him, Rabbi thou art the Son of God: thou art the King of Israel" (John 1:49).

Thinking It Over

1. How is Christ instructing you? In what way can you make more time to sit at his feet and learning from him? What things might you be learning from the world's heroes, movie stars and financial experts instead of from Jesus?,

2. Why do you need the one-time sacrifice of Jesus on the cross? What does the Bible say about people who think they are pretty good and do not need to be saved from anything? him alone for salvation? Why do you need the one-time sacrifice of Jesus Christ on the cross? ,

3. How are you showing that Jesus Christ is the King of your life and that you are bowing before him and obeying his rules? In what ways are you showing that you are King of your life?

Comfort Ye My People

Comfort ye, comfort ye my people, saith your God. Speak ye comfortably to Jerusalem, and cry unto her, that her warfare is accomplished, that her iniquity is pardoned: for she hath received of the Lord's hand double for all her sins.
—Isaiah 40:1–3

Messiah begins with soft, tender strokes from the orchestra that communicate peace and consolation. Confidently the tenor soloist sings a short, pithy phrase: "Comfort ye," and the orchestra echoes him. Gradually the soloist introduces more of the biblical text: "Comfort ye my people . . . saith your God. Speak ye comfortably to Jerusalem." *Messiah* is an anthem celebrating the only comfort that Christians possess.

The repetition in Isaiah 40:1 "Comfort ye, comfort ye" places an emphasis on the tremendous need for God's preachers to bring comfort to the covenant people. John the Baptist needed to bring a message of comfort. Christ preached a message of comfort.

The English word *comfort* has the word *fort* in it. It is related to the word *fortress*, a strong, fortified place. This reminds us that the Christian comfort is a strong consolation. We comfort someone by bringing solace and encouragement when they are hurting.

In Isaiah, God tells His prophet to cry to His people. The message is important and should be shouted. The shouted message is twofold: first, Jerusalem's warfare is accomplished; and second, her iniquities are pardoned.

The Messiah has conquered our enemies. He has fought for us and overcome death. He triumphed over the Devil. He made a show of His enemies—and triumphed over them at the cross. In principle, Christ has defeated the kingdom of Satan. He will return to mop up the battlefield, so we are delivered from our enemies.

The amazing news of the gospel is that our iniquities are pardoned. The word *iniquity* points to the guilt that our sin incurs. Sin has left us in need of comfort. Our first parents, Adam and Eve, sinned, and the entire human race has been burdened with the guilt of Adam. We are born sinners and remain sinners till death. We are unable, by nature, to escape sin and hell.

We need comfort because we know that by nature we add to our guilt. Not only do we carry the guilt of Adam; we personally sin against God every day. I find that I am more concerned about myself than the glory of God. I do not love the Lord my God with all my heart, soul, and mind. My heart is often divided. Besides this, the love I show to my neighbor is so small. God commands me to love my neighbor as myself, but I am caught up with my own selfish needs. The longer I live, the more I increase the debt I owe God.

The effects of sin are found around the world. Physical pain, sickness, death, storms, and destruction are present everywhere. Humans everywhere are crying out in pain. But it is only God who can bring the comfort they need. You need comfort today as you go about your daily duties, and you will need comfort when you take your last breath in death.

The first word in *Messiah* is "comfort." Almost two hundred years earlier than Handel, Zacharius Ursinus and Caspar Olevianus wrote the Heidelberg Catechism for young people, and it contains the same theme of comfort with which *Messiah* begins.

There is only one possible comfort for people living in the miserable condition of sin. The soloist reveals how comfort can be found. God has pardoned the iniquity of His people. The warfare with sin is accomplished. The Messiah has dealt with our sin and guilt. He has conquered the Devil. Our iniquity has been pardoned. The Lord

Himself has given us pardon. He grants to those given to Him by the Father the righteousness of Christ. Christians receive double for all their sins.

Acknowledge your sin before God and look to Jesus as the only way for sin to be forgiven and to find lasting comfort. Since you are a prophet, priest, and king; you can read God's Word of comfort and let His peace wash over your soul. You can speak comfort to yourself and to those in distress. Be a friend who gives comfort to others.

Thinking It Over

1. Write out the answer to the first question in the Heidelberg Catechism: "What is your only comfort in life and death?" (You can find this online if you don't own a copy: https://threeforms.org/heidelberg-catechism/.)

2. Comfort begins by knowing your sin. David found this to be true. Write down and memorize Psalm 51:3.

3. God brought David comfort through confession. What sin did David confess in Psalm 51? (See 2 Samuel 11).

4. People often run to things that mask the guilt of sin, instead of running to Jesus Christ. They run from those who hold them responsible. They run to alcohol that gives momentary freedom from guilt, they take drugs which temporarily covers shame. Where are you going for comfort? Why?

Every Valley Shall Be Exalted

The voice of him that crieth in the wilderness, Prepare ye the way of the LORD, make straight in the desert a highway for our God. Every valley shall be exalted, and every mountain and hill shall be made low: and the crooked shall be made straight, and the rough places plain.
—Isaiah 40:3–4

The resounding voice of the tenor soloist sings about one who would come crying in the wilderness. A young man, John the Baptist, lived in the wilderness eating locust and wild honey (Matthew 3:4). Jesus identifies John as the one crying in the wilderness.

John the Baptist cried in the wilderness that the Israelites must prepare the way of the Lord (Matthew 3:3). God Himself was coming in the person of Jesus Christ. The Israelites were commanded to "believe the gospel" and "repent." This preparation for the Messiah was pictured in terms of preparing a road. God's people are called to labor-intensive work like that of building and leveling a road.

When the president comes to a city, the city government makes sure that the presidential limousine does not ride on a bumpy road full of potholes. Preparation is made to ensure that the road is smooth and straight. We need to prepare the way for Christ by repenting of our sins.

Isaiah mentions well-known landforms: valleys, mountains, and hills. The deep sunken areas as well as the more extreme heights will be brought to the level of the plains. In preparation for the entry of the King of kings, an entire landscape makeover is needed. A cosmetic touchup is unacceptable. Valleys need to be filled in; mountains and hills need to be leveled; crooked roads must be straightened up; and rough places need to smoothed out. This road building symbolizes repentance. No area of one's life may be overlooked or ignored. My crooked living needs straightening, and the rough places of my life must become smooth.

John's great privilege is to announce the King's coming. Many Israelites were in a wilderness. Their lives were dry and like a desert. John calls them to refreshment by way of repentance and faith in Christ. The way of preparation for the Lord is the way of repentance. "Repent, for the kingdom of heaven is at hand" (Matthew 3:2) Mere regret will not do. True sorrow includes being broken and contrite of heart (Psalm 51:17). Sin should not be quickly brushed aside, laughed about, or treated flippantly. Sin is repulsive atrocity against God. We must run to God, seeking His mercy and forgiveness.

"Repent!" This is the message of John the Baptist. Repentance is a turning away from sin and a desire to live a new and godly life. Repentance involves agreeing with God that you have broken His righteous commandments. The Holy Spirit enables us to repent. He convicts us of our sin and causes us to recoil from evil.
A repentant heart desires to turn from sin and follow Christ. God's forgiveness washes away the sins of the vilest offender. God can change the deepest darkest valley into a pleasant plain! Repent!

Thinking It Over

1. List three sins of which you need to repent.

2.　Describe the nature of your repentance. How does repentance manifest itself in your life? When was the last time that you repented of a sin?

3.　What idols are you in danger of erecting this week? How can you topple them over?

And the Glory of the Lord

And the glory of the LORD shall be revealed, and all flesh shall see it together:
for the mouth of the LORD has spoken it.
—Isaiah 40:5

The glory of the Lord shall be revealed! Handel uses the music and words to communicate an unveiling effect. Just as wrapping paper gradually reveals the gift inside, God's glory will be seen. Again and again the words "And the glory of the Lord shall be revealed" are sung. Closer and closer we come to the day when we will see!

Isaiah sees the birth of Jesus and His second coming at the end of time as if they are one event. It is much like seeing a huge storm coming. When dark, billowing clouds approach and the wind picks up, you know it's going to rain. You are unable to decipher the length of the storm, the amount of rain, and which part of your town will be inundated by floodwaters. You only know it is going to rain. Both the coming of the Messiah and His second coming are part of the end of history. Isaiah sees Christ coming. He foresees that His glory will be exhibited. Although Isaiah may not be able to decipher between the Messiah coming to Bethlehem and His second coming on the clouds of glory, He foresees the coming of Jesus.

Isaiah wants his hearers to know that this prophecy did not originate with him. God has revealed this: "for the mouth of the LORD hath spoken" (Isaiah 40:5). Perk up your ears and listen when God speaks!

God's glory is the shining forth of His majesty and purity. It is not a momentary characteristic that appears and then fades. It radiates from His divine essence. Since man is so small compared to the planets and stars above him, he should worship the glorious God who hung the solar system and galaxies. When man looks up into the spacious heavens, he should hear, "the heavens declare the glory of God; and the firmament sheweth his handywork" (Psalm 19:1).

At Mount Sinai, God's glory was so encompassing, filling the tabernacle, that Moses was not even able to enter. When Moses was on the mountain in Exodus 24:17, he described God's glory: "And the sight of the glory of the LORD was like devouring fire on the top of the mount in the eyes of the children of Israel."

A few shepherds on the outskirts of Bethlehem beheld the glory of God. Luke states it this way: "And, lo, the angel of the Lord came upon them, and the glory of the Lord shone round about them: and they were sore afraid" (Luke 2:9). What a spectacular evening the shepherds experienced! God met with shepherds who had low social status and favored them with a moment of unforgettable wonder.

Imagine walking beside the Lord daily for several years as the apostle John did. He recognized Jesus as the only begotten Son of the Father. He realized that Jesus was begotten, not created. John said, "We beheld his glory, the glory as of the only begotten of the Father, full of grace and truth" (John 1:14).

As New Testament believers, we look back two thousand years to the birth of Jesus. We look ahead to His *parousia*, or second coming. Although Jesus's first coming was in lowliness, His second coming will be with pomp and splendor. God's glory will be displayed at the second coming: "For as the lightning cometh out of the east, and shineth even unto the west; so shall also the coming of the Son of Man be" (Matthew 24:27). Christ's glory will be displayed universally. Everyone across the continents will see the divine glory of the returning Christ

Thinking It Over

1. What is the glory of God?

2. What aspect of God's glory are you most anxious to see?

3. Why did God's glory intimidate biblical characters?

Thus Saith the Lord

*For thus saith the LORD of hosts; Yet once, it is a little while, and
I will shake the heavens, and the earth, and the sea, and the dry land;
and I will shake all nations, and the desire of all nations shall come:
and I will fill this house with glory, saith the LORD of hosts.*
—Haggai 2:6–7

*Behold, I will send my messenger, and he shall prepare the way before me:
and the LORD, whom ye seek, shall suddenly come to his temple, even the
messenger of the covenant, whom ye delight in: behold, he shall come,
saith the LORD of hosts.*
—Malachi 3:1

With great confidence and conviction, the bass soloist states, "Thus saith the Lord, the Lord of Hosts." God calmly sits in heaven bringing to pass His good pleasure. The calm confidence of the words makes a huge contrast to the agitated sixteenth notes that express the shaking of the heaven and earth. Our world is shaken up regularly by the unexpected events God brings to pass.

The prophet begins by stating that God has spoken. The exalted Lord to whom the armies of heaven bow has spoken! Listen with care! Give your attention! Focus! He has a message that He wants you to hear. God no longer speaks audibly today, but He speaks through His written word, the Bible. Revelation 22:18–19 warns us about adding to the Scriptures. We have the complete word of God. Let us treasure it, read it, and obey it.

Throughout history, major events have shaken our world: the curse, the flood, the Tower of Babel, and the Red Sea crossing. These shakings continue in the form of pandemics, tsunamis, fire, earthquakes, and flooding. The earth and its citizens have felt the impact of these events. There is one huge coming event that will shake the heavens and earth for a final time. John alludes to this in the book of Revelation when he describes how the earth will be shaken, the sun will be darkened, the moon will become red like blood, and the stars will fall from the places. All this will signal the return of the Desire of the Nations.

When the weary Jewish captives of Babylon arrived back in the land of Judah, they found Solomon's temple burned and destroyed. They made their first order of business to build homes for themselves. Unfortunately, God's house lay neglected. Haggai reprimanded them and commanded them to take up the great task of building God's house. He motivated them to this work with a promise that "the desire of all nations shall come"!

After hundreds of years of silence, John the Baptist had the privilege to preach the arrival of the Desired One. Jesus Christ, the Desired One, suddenly arrived at the temple in the week after His birth. Mary and Joseph made the six-mile trip from Bethlehem to Jerusalem to present Him to the Lord. The aged Simeon came to the temple and took up Baby Jesus in his arms and blessed God for His provision of salvation. The eighty-four-year-old Anna, who had been waiting for the redemption of Jerusalem, also celebrated the coming of the Messiah.

This Jesus, who arrived suddenly at the temple, proclaims God's covenant. He is the way of salvation. All history culminates in the salvation He brings. God's promises throughout the whole Bible are fulfilled in Jesus Christ.

Jesus is the great hope of the elect who are found in every nation on earth. We live in exciting times when we see God gathering

His elect from nations around the globe. He is gathering a church in Muslim countries and in China and North Korea. Christ is the desire of elect sinners who populate the nations of this world.

When we call Jesus "the desire of nations," this implies a longing for Him. When elect sinners are converted, they long for Jesus. They desire the salvation that is found in Him. He is the one we hunger and thirst after. We want Him to come again and make all things right. We want to know Him intimately and sit at His feet like Mary did. We want to know Him with the familiarity that the apostle John enjoyed as he rested upon His bosom. We want His hand to rest on our covenant children, as He blessed the little lambs many years ago.

We desire Jesus's return. We can't wait for the day when we will see Him in all His glory! It is our passion to know Him and the power of His resurrection. There is one thing the psalmist desired: "One thing have I desired of the LORD, that will I seek after; that I may dwell in the house of the LORD all the days of my life, to behold the beauty of the LORD and to enquire in his temple" (Psalm 27:4).

Thinking It Over

1. Have you ever felt an earthquake? How did it effect you?

2. How will God once more shake the heavens and the earth? What will happen?

3. What does it mean that Jesus is the "desire of the nations"?

4. Do you long after God? Do you desire to be in His presence? How is this evident? Or not evident?

5. Do you desire the return of the king? What actions of yours demonstrate this?

But Who May Abide the Day

But who may abide the day of his coming? and who shall stand when he appeareth? for he is like a refiner's fire, and like fullers' soap.
—Malachi 3:2

When the heavens, the earth, the sea, and the dry land are shaken by the Lord, where will you be found? Under whose shadow will you abide? Handel cleverly uses the bass soloist to ask an important question that demands an immediate answer. He asks, "But who may abide the day of His coming?"

After this question the music takes on a quick tempo. The speed and power lead us to contemplate life's brevity and how quickly we will meet Christ as judge. The Lord will appear! He will come on the clouds of heaven as a refiner's fire. He will publicly declare the righteousness of believers. But He will also pronounce that wicked unbelievers are condemned.

What man, woman, young adult, or child envisions that they are pure enough to stand before God when He appears at the close of history? Only those who are arrogant or ignorant will make such a claim, for no sinful person can withstand God's judgments. No sinner can stand in the presence of the Judge of all the earth and be found not guilty. No sinful son of Adam can withstand the fury of the divine wrath unleashed on a rebellious creature.

When the Lord shook the earth at the time of Noah, He spared only eight souls in the ark. So it will be that in the last judgment only those covered by the blood of Christ will abide the day of His coming.

Jesus is coming back again! This time He comes in judgment. The righteous judge will send us either to heaven or to hell. How will that last day find you? Will you be able to stand and defend yourself and your deeds before the perfect and righteous Judge? Will you sustain the perfect scrutiny of every detail of your life?

"Who may abide the day of His coming? And who shall stand when He appears?" The question is rhetorical, and it answers itself: no one. No king, no ruler, no adult, no child, or no infant can stand before the righteous Judge in themselves. No one apart from Christ will be able to endure His second coming.

Do you think you are a pretty good person? Do you suppose that you are kind and generous and loving? You might wonder why you need to be covered by someone else's righteousness. Maybe you think that you are a good neighbor. Do you think that you are congenial and compliant? But God requires perfection. He requires that His creatures love their neighbors as themselves. He requires that His creatures love God Himself with all their heart, soul, mind, and strength. You and I are not perfect—far from it.

Paul says in Romans 3:10–11, "There is none righteous, no not one: there is none that understandeth, there is none that seeketh after God." The reason why you and I cannot stand by ourselves is that we have "all gone out of the way" and "become unprofitable." God's Word says that "there is none that does good, no, not one" (Rom. 3:12). Apart from being born again, not a one of us fallen sons or daughters of Adam do something that is truly good—that is, out of faith in God and directed to the glory of God. When you do outwardly good things but do not do them to the glory of God, they are not good works.

Paul tells us that "there is no fear of God before their eyes" (Rom. 3:18). We must come to realize how sinful we are. If the righteous Judge were to look at you or me apart from Jesus Christ, He would see only sin and filth.

We humans are notorious for justifying our actions and imagining ourselves as better than we really are. We deceive ourselves. If you possess such a high opinion of yourself, beg the Lord to show you your sin. Read your Bible and ask God to reveal His purity and magnificent holiness to you.

The notes and sounds Handel uses to describe Christ as a refiner's fire are like brush strokes on a canvas. As the music speeds up, we can envision sparks flying, flames leaping, and a hot fire. A refiner's fire burned hot at over 1,947 degrees Fahrenheit. As a refiner's fire, Christ consumes the wicked and purifies and sanctifies elect sinners.

The heat of the fire is so intense that it burns away impurities. When Christ comes, He will purify the sons of Levi. He will burn away the weaknesses and sins in the lives of elect priests. God is so pure that He cannot stand sin. He will not allow sinners to dwell in His presence.

Fuller's soap is not ordinary soap but a cleansing soap known for its extraordinary ability to take grease and grime from wool, making the fibers pure and clean. Who is it that may abide the day of His coming? All those who have been purified by the refiner and purifier. Christ sanctifies elect sinners.

He takes guilty sinners and purifies them! Christ takes those whom the Father has given Him before the foundation of the earth and forgives all their sin through His shed blood. All evil is eradicated and total pardon given. Not only will things be removed from their life but they will be whiter than snow.

Thinking It Over

1. What is "fuller's soap"? Why does the prophet mention this soap?

2. What is the significance of being able to stand when Christ appears? What is involved in this standing?

3. Psalm 130:4 states, "If thou, LORD, shouldest mark iniquities, O Lord, who shall stand?" What does it mean that God might "mark iniquities"?

4. Psalm 130:5 says "But there is forgiveness with thee, that thou mayest be feared." What does it mean to fear God? Why should you fear Him?

And He Shall Purify

And he shall sit as a refiner and purifier of silver: and he shall purify the sons of Levi, and purge them as gold and silver, that they may offer unto the Lord an offering in righteousness.
—Malachi 3:3

The deep sound of the bass soloist is interrupted by a melodious response from the chorus. They answer the question: Who may abide the day of His coming? The choir sings about how Christ will purify the sons of Levi so that they can offer sacrifices to the Lord in righteousness. My Refiner promises to purify His priests. The magnitude of this promise overwhelms me. Its truth tugs at my heart. God incarnate will rescue the sons of Levi.

The text of Scripture from which this chorus originates is in the book of Malachi. The sons of Levi were the priests and their male offspring, the descendants of Aaron. God gave this family the special duty of serving Him in the temple. It was their calling to offer sacrifices to the Lord.

God was angry because the priests had been offering animals that were lame, sick, blind, and even stolen. Sacrificing a lamb was a picture of Jesus, the perfect Son of God, who would sacrifice Himself on the cross for our sins. The Levites made a mockery of Jesus by accepting blemished animals to be sacrificed. The sons of Levi were not treasuring Jesus Christ, whose perfect sacrifice was pictured in those offerings.

Besides that, they did not trust the Almighty. They questioned whether God could provide for their needs. Disbelief led them to hold back their gifts. Not wanting to come up short, they withheld their offerings from Him. God reprimanded them for robbery.

The Levites played a negative role in this problematic worship. They accepted the sick and blemished animals that people brought to be sacrificed. That is why the sons of Levi needed to be refined. Gold and silver need refinement because they are usually found mixed with other minerals. Refining separates the gold and silver from the other minerals. The process begins by crushing the minerals into powder and then applying heat until they become liquid. The dross, or impurity, is removed from the top of the cauldron. The process demands continual watching. If the heat were to exceed the degree necessary for refining, it would turn the gold or silver to ash.

Jesus, the Messenger of the covenant, is our refiner. He sits at God's right hand refining sons of Levi. Since He will not allow them to be consumed, He stays attentive throughout the refining process as He burns away sin. He takes the sons of Levi with all their impurities and purifies them. He applies His refining fire at just the right temperature so as not to consume those He purifies. Christ sends fiery trials to sanctify His people. He suffered His entire life and gave Himself to die on the cross in order to refine the sons of Levi and all His elect people. This was a costly sacrifice.

Today, God's people are a kingdom of priests (Revelation 1:6). We have the priestly office and are the spiritual sons of Levi. In Numbers 8:14, 16-17 God says that "the Levites shall be mine.... For they are wholly given unto me from among the children of Israel...have I taken them unto me. For all the firstborn of all the children of Israel are mine."

The priests of old offered lambs to God whereas we now offer sacrifices of praise. Although we are no longer commanded to offer sacrifices for our sin, we are told to confess our sins to God in prayer. As priests we have the high calling to offer prayers on behalf of brothers and sisters in Christ. We pray for those who do not yet know Christ that they would come to know His saving grace.

Our purification results in us offering pleasing sacrifices to God. Having been sanctified by Christ, we walk in good works. Although we must wait for the new heavens and new earth for our total refining to be manifest, already now God is stripping away our impurities. We come to hate our selfishness and desire to live for the glory of Christ. We no longer want to question God's perfect plan but seek to trust Him fully. By God's grace and His refinement of us, we choose to give offerings in righteousness to the Lord. "For then I will I turn to the people a pure language, that they may all call upon the name of the Lord, to serve him with one consent" (Zephaniah 3:9).

Thinking It Over

1. Our personal refining can take place in many areas of our lives. It can occur through singleness, financial hardship, health issues, old age, and many other situations. In what areas of your life are you experiencing refining? Write about the refining process you are experiencing.

2. Has the purifying process been difficult? Explain how.

3. The goal of the purifying process is an offering of praise for what God has done in your life. What role is praise playing in your life?

Behold! A Virgin Shall Conceive

Therefore the Lord himself shall give you a sign; behold, a virgin shall conceive, and bear a son, and shall call his name Immanuel.
—Isaiah 7:14

Behold, a virgin shall be with child, and shall bring forth a son, and they shall call his name Emmanuel, which being interpreted is, God with us.
—Matthew 1:23

Next, we hear the voice of an alto. Handel wrote a recitative in which the soloist sing-speaks the words as the orchestra accompanies in a very minimal way: "Therefore the Lord himself shall give you a sign; behold, a virgin shall conceive, and bear a son, and shall call His name Immanuel."

The virgin birth is the sign spoken of by the prophet Isaiah and fulfilled in Matthew. Do you remember the story? While Ahaz was king in Judah, the kings of Syria and Israel instigated war against Judah. When Ephraim joined Syria, fear seized Ahaz and the people of Judah. The prophet Isaiah is told to meet Ahaz and tell him not to fear: "Thus saith the Lord GOD, It shall not stand, neither shall it come to pass" (Isaiah 7:7).

Ahaz is instructed to ask a sign of God, but he would not! But God gave a sign: "Behold, a virgin shall conceive, and bear a son, and shall call his name Immanuel" (Isaiah 7:14). This prophecy pointed to the birth of Jesus.

This event spoken of in the opening chapter of the Gospel of Matthew is our focus. Luke gives us the details. An angel named Gabriel visited a young virgin. The Holy Spirit came on Mary, and a child was conceived within her womb apart from a physical relationship with a man. From this miraculous conception, a baby boy would be born.

Immanuel is my favorite title for Jesus. "God with us" communicates the wonder of how God dwells in His Son, who unites Himself to a human nature. Immanuel speaks of the incarnation. Jesus is God and has taken on flesh and dwelt among us. God incarnate, Jesus Christ, lived among the Israelites. He is still with us by His Holy Spirit. Immanuel lives and reigns today.

The name Immanuel emphasizes the close relationship we have with God through Jesus Christ. This title magnifies the covenant God has with His people. Just as the Israelites were guided by the pillar of cloud and the pillar of fire as they left Egypt, so we have the Lord always with us to guide us.

David confesses this in Psalm 139:7–12:

> Whither shall I go from thy spirit? or whither shall I flee from thy presence? If I ascend up into heaven, thou art there: if I make my bed in hell, behold, thou art there. If I take the wings of the morning, and dwell in the uttermost parts of the sea; even there shall thy hand lead me, and thy right hand shall hold me. If I say, Surely the darkness shall cover me; even the night shall be light about me. Yea, the darkness hideth not from thee; but the night shineth as the day: the darkness and the light are both alike to thee.

Immanuel is with me . . .

when my heart is bursting with joy.

when someone I love dies.

when I sin and confess my transgressions.

when no one realizes the burden I carry.

when I am in pain.

when I am sad.

when I need wisdom and guidance.

when I am confused and don't know what to do.

when I am reading His Word.

when my work is overwhelming.

when I am worshiping in church.

when my friends forsake me,

God is with me, Immanuel.

Thinking It Over

1. Add three lines of your own to the confession above.

    a. Immanuel is with me, when I

    b. Immanuel is with me, when I

    c. Immanuel is with me, when I

2. What does the name Immanuel mean?

3. What is a virgin? Why must Christ be born of a virgin?

4. Write out Matthew 28:20. How is this verse good news for Christians?

5. Write out Revelation 21:3. How does this passage give comfort?

Thou That Tellest Good Tidings

O Zion, that bringest good tidings, get thee up into the high mountain;
O Jerusalem, that bringest good tidings, lift up thy voice with strength; lift it
up, be not afraid; say unto the cities of Judah, Behold your God!
—Isaiah 40:9

The 1611 edition of the King James Version (KJV) contains a marginal reading that provides an alternate translation of Isaiah 40:9. The actual text of the KJV read, "O Zion, that bringest good tidings, get thee up into the high mountain." This translation identifies Zion as the active one bringing good tidings. The marginal reading, however, says, "O thou that tellest good tidings to Zion." This conveys the idea that someone else is telling good tidings to Zion. Jennens, Handel's lyricist, chose the marginal reading as the text for this song.

John Newton penned the words, "glorious things of the are spoken, Zion, city of our God." It is the beautiful city of God, the hill on which the temple was built. The names Zion and Jerusalem are used interchangeably as we speak about the place where God dwells. The city of Jerusalem is elevated from the surrounding area as what geographers call a tableland. It is located thirty-seven miles east of the Mediterranean Sea.

Not only was Jerusalem a beautiful city in Israel but it was where God chose to dwell with His people. The city of Jerusalem is symbolic of the church of the living God since the elect are His dwelling place. The Lord has chosen Zion as the place of His delight. Believers in Christ are His Zion.

How delightful to know that "there shall yet old men and old women dwell in the streets of Jerusalem, and every man with his staff in his hand for very age. And the streets of the city shall be full of boys and girls playing in the streets thereof" (Zechariah 8:4–5). The city will be full and the variety great. God tells His people: "Behold, I will save my people from the east country, and from the west country; and I will bring them, and they shall dwell in the midst of Jerusalem: and they shall be my people, and I will be their God, in truth and righteousness" (vv. 7–8).

The church of God has exceeding great tidings to bring. We have not been left in our sin! For those in Christ separation from God in hell has been replaced with the promise of a magnificent city in which "the Lord God Almighty and the Lamb are the temple of it" (Revelation 21:22).

What must the church of the living God do with these "good tidings"? Is it a secret for the "in" group? Is it something to be embarrassed or ashamed about? Is it just for clean-cut people? Is it just for the people of one race? Ten thousand times I say no! These good tidings must be spoken by us with courage and delight. They are worth shouting from mountaintops. We must hold no energy back as we proclaim what God has done. These "good tidings" are nothing to be embarrassed about. This is the best news humans have ever heard. We must replace any fear with joy and boldness.

The gospel message multiplies! Rejoice as you tell others the good tidings! Those with whom you share the message must tell their acquaintances. In this way the gospel message multiplies until the whole world knows the good tidings of salvation. The prerequisite to Jesus's second coming is that "the gospel must first be published among all nations" (Mark 13:10).

Our God saves! "Thus saith the LORD; I am returned unto Zion, and will dwell in the midst of Jerusalem: and Jerusalem shall be called a city of truth; and the mountain of the LORD of hosts the holy mountain" (Zechariah 8:3).

Thinking It Over

1. What is Zion?

2. Why should Zion say, "Behold your God"? What is going on that motivates Zion to say this? To whom is she saying it?

3. As disciples of Jesus Christ, we have exceedingly great tidings to tell. Write a personal account of what God through Jesus Christ has done for you. Next time an opportunity arises, do not give way to fear. Share your story.

For Behold, Darkness

*For, behold, the darkness shall cover the earth, and gross darkness
the people: but the LORD shall arise upon thee, and his glory shall be seen
upon thee. And the Gentiles shall come to thy light, and kings to the
brightness of thy rising.*
—Isaiah 60:2–3

Handel mysteriously portrays darkness by beginning with slow, downward tones. The notes give an eerie feeling. The bass soloist reaches down and then even further down to the word *earth*. Then the notes rise, and everything changes with the arrival of God's glory. The arpeggio centers on the word *glory* and brings us to new heights.

Planet Earth is a place of spiritual darkness. In the Bible sin and evil are pictured as darkness. When we sin, we walk in darkness. John says, "Men loved darkness rather than light, because their deeds were evil. For every one that doeth evil hateth the light, neither cometh to the light, lest his deeds should be reproved" (John 3:19–20). What John said is true. Advertisers lure people using words like *evil*, *vile*, and *wicked*. Why? People apart from Christ are drawn to what is base and corrupt.

The works of darkness are manifest in a denial of God as creator, life giver, and king. Apart from Jesus Christ, people will not bow the knee to the King of kings. Human beings want to be their own king and call the shots. God gives such people over to a reprobate mind. In Romans 1:29–31, Paul lists sins of darkness as "unrighteousness, fornication, wickedness, covetousness, maliciousness; full of envy, murder, debate, deceit, malignity; whisperers, backbiters, haters of God, despiteful, proud, boasters, inventors of evil things, disobedient to parents, without understanding, covenantbreakers, without natural affection, implacable, unmerciful."

Since darkness has not been totally eradicated from our lives, sin will continue to lurk within us until death. We will find ourselves daily fighting against sins that rise up against our wills.

The covenant people received the beautiful prophecy that they would not be left in darkness because Messiah would come. Today we celebrate Jesus, the light of the world. He is pure and holy, "and in him is no darkness at all" (1 John 1:5).

God predicted in Isaiah that Gentiles would worship the Christ: "And the Gentiles shall come to the light." (Isaiah 60:3). After the birth of Jesus, Gentile Magi traveled to Bethlehem from the East to worship the newborn king. Today the Christian church is made up of thousands of Gentile believers. We can celebrate God's grace in sending the light of the gospel to people like you and I. Former Islamic Gentiles in Toronto have turned from Islam to Jesus Christ. God is calling Gentile gang members out of the darkness of sin while still behind prison bars.

Thinking It Over

1. What does it mean that "darkness will cover the earth"?

2. Where will this "gross" darkness be located?

3. What is the glory of God?

4. How will the glory of the Lord be seen?

5. Who were the first Gentiles to come to the light?

The People That Walked in Darkness

The people that walked in darkness have seen a great light: they that dwell in the land of the shadow of death, upon them hath the light shined.
—Isaiah 9:2

The goal of a good fiction writer is to describe things in such a way without specifically stating the case so that the reader will understand. "Show, don't tell," is the motto of novelists. A good novelist demonstrates the joy of the main character through his or her actions and speech and doesn't merely tell you that the person is happy.

Hundreds of years ago Handel employed this method. He allowed the music to "show" the excitement of the text. He employed many tones and rhythms to convey ideas. He showed without telling (with words). In this piece, Handel uses the bass note to communicate the effect of walking in darkness.

At about two in the morning, my dogs began barking to go outside. I carefully walked through my dark house. I didn't want to wake the children. Then "bang!" I stumbled into a corner table. A little clock crashed onto the floor. Walking in the darkness was unwise. I couldn't see where I was going. The effect was a broken clock.

Anything that deviates from God's perfect truth and holiness is pictured as dark and sinful. "God is light, and in him is no darkness at all" (1 John 1:5). Many of the people in this region of Israel went about their lives "in the dark." They lived in disobedience to the God of the covenant. They lived depraved lives, just like the Gentiles. Many Israelites were hypocrites. They could talk the talk about worshiping Jehovah God. But they lived for the things of this world. It was covenant people who lived in the northern part of Palestine, in the land of Zebulun and Naphtali, who walked in darkness.

When Pekah, the son of Remaliah, reigned over Israel, he continued in the sin of the kings before him. God raised up Tiglath-pileser, king of Assyria, to judge the kingdom of Israel. The Bible tells us what Tiglath-pileser did with the Israelites dwelling in the north. He attacked "Galilee, all the land of Naphtali, and carried them captive to Assyria" (2 Kings 15:29). These were extremely dark days for the covenant people in the north.

After Joseph, Mary, and Jesus fled to Egypt, they came back to Israel and lived in Nazareth (Matthew 2:23). The city of Nazareth was in the tribal territory of Zebulun. Later, at age twelve, Jesus submitted himself to his parents' authority in their hometown of Nazareth (Luke 2:51). The apostle Matthew tells us, "And leaving Nazareth, [Jesus] came and dwelt in Capernaum, which is upon the sea coast, in the borders of Zabulon and Nephthalim" (Matthew 4:13).

The city of Capernaum, where Jesus spent much time during His ministry, was a city also located in Naphtali. Jesus taught in the synagogues of Capernaum and healed many of the sick in the city.

Centuries before the Messiah lived in the tribal areas of Naphtali, Isaiah predicted that a great light would come to this region. This area was populated by Jews and Gentiles. Just to the north lay the pagan country of Syria. Their heathen gods, pagan culture, and strange customs would have a great influence on this region. Syria became a center of Hellenistic influence. Therefore, the Greek gods and Hellenistic culture from Syria influenced the north of Palestine. A trade route that cut through Zebulun and Naphtali brought a variety of influence into the area. Traders brought Hellenistic culture, idolatry, and more to the region.

Jesus Christ is the great light! He walked onto the stage of history as a little boy and accompanied his biological mother, Mary, and his adoptive father, Joseph, to Nazareth. At age thirty Jesus began to shine as He proclaimed that the kingdom of God was at hand. Covenant people who lived in the region of Zebulun and Naphtali were the first to hear that the time had come.

Jesus's life shone with holiness and truth. Through His preaching and mighty miracles, a light began to shine. He was visible to elect sinners who had walked in darkness. They had lived in hopelessness, but hope had arrived.

Jesus's light is not dim. He is not like a flashlight with dead batteries. This light is a great light. His light lets us see danger zones, pits, depths, cracks, and twists in the darkness. The greater the illumination in a room, the greater ability we possess to see spots and dirt. When the late afternoon sun shines in my western windows, I see dirt that had been invisible. I discover that my windows are filthy. I see layers of dust on tables and little dust bunnies under chairs. Light reveals what we could not otherwise see. In order to see our sin and know our need for Jesus Christ, he must shine the light of the gospel into our life. By nature, we are blind to sin and unable to understand God's perfect holiness.

Not only do the people lie in darkness but over them lies "the shadow of death." Death is all around us. Men who are muscular and fit slump over on their desks and die of heart attacks. Young women suffer fatal injuries in car accidents. Children drown in pools. Babies die in the womb and are brought into the world stillborn. Ducklings are eaten by raccoons. Everything decays. Blue-green patches of mold grow on my homemade bread. Red geraniums shrivel up. We dwell in the land of the shadow of death. People die daily. Every second two people die.

The light of Jesus Christ breaks through this darkness. The Sun of Righteousness arises in the north. He reveals the tremendous grace of God toward penitent sinners. Christ raises the dead to show that He is the resurrection and the life. It was prophesied, "He will swallow up death in victory; and the Lord GOD will wipe away tears from off all faces; and the rebuke of his people shall he take away from off all the earth: for the LORD has spoken" (Isaiah 25:8).

Thinking It Over

1. How did the inhabitants of Zebulun and Naphtali live in darkness?

2. Why is this dark place called the land of the "shadow of death"?

For unto Us a Child Is Born

For unto us a child is born, unto us a son is given: and the government shall
be upon his shoulder: and his name shall be called Wonderful, Counsellor,
The mighty God, The everlasting Father, The Prince of Peace.
—Isaiah 9:6

A child's birth is an exciting time. The virgin Mary gave birth to a child in an extraordinary way. The Holy Spirit came upon her, and through His overshadowing her He brought about the miracle of the incarnation. Mary became pregnant without a sexual union. In obedience to the decree of Caesar Augustus, she traveled to the city of Bethlehem and there delivered her firstborn son. Since the town was crowded with visitors who were also registering to be taxed, there was no room in the inn. Mary gave birth in a stable and laid the sinless Son of God in a manger!

In the incarnation of the Son of God, the God of the covenant shows His love for His people, God gives His Son. Our God is a generous God. He knows our needs. As a wonderful Father, He provides for us. We sometimes give gifts to people who love us. When we were yet enemies of God and hated Him, He gave us, His elect people, the gift of His only begotten Son.

Long ago, Isaiah predicted the birth of the baby born in Bethlehem. In Isaiah 9, under the inspiration of the Holy Spirit, Isaiah saw Jesus, the Son of God, hundreds of years before His birth. By faith we also recognize the extraordinary person who was born in Bethlehem.

Isaiah gave high titles to the promised Messiah. Only the Son of God in human flesh can possess such wonderful titles that befit the King of glory.

The resurrected and ascended Christ is the King of glory. His exalted state and mighty power is at work in the governance of the world. Who of us could imagine ruling a nation, much less the cosmos? Jesus presides with sovereign power over all things. The governance of the earth, the planets, the sun, the moon, and one hundred billion galaxies rests on the shoulders of the One born in Bethlehem. "The government shall be upon His shoulders," the ancient prophet said.

What title or titles could befit someone as glorious as the messianic King?

The music that Handel puts with the lyrics, "For unto us a child is born," is happy and celebrative.

Then the chorus celebrates the titles of the Messiah. A loud exuberant crescendo of exulting praise circulates throughout the auditorium as the choir sings, "Wonderful, Counselor, the mighty God, the Everlasting Father, the Prince of Peace."

The first title given to Messiah is "Wonderful Counselor." There is some question about whether this is one title or two. It is quite clear that for the next titles, two words go together. Christ is "the mighty God." He is "Everlasting Father." But it is not clear whether "Wonderful" is a title that stands by itself or whether it modifies the title "Counselor." I think that we can understand it both ways. The word *Wonderful* is striking because it has connotations of deity by itself. When the Angel of Jehovah appeared in the Old Testament, Manoah asked His name. Samson's father asked: "What is thy name, that when thy sayings come to pass we may do thee honour?" (Judges 13:17). The Angel of Jehovah responded by questioning this request, saying: "Why askest thou thus after my name, seeing it is secret?"

(Judges 13:18) The word for "secret" is the same word that is translated "wonderful." The first title of Christ is "Wonderful" because He is, in the incarnation, evidence of the greatest wonder of all—the wonder of God becoming man.

Christ is also given the title "Counselor." A counselor gives guidance to those in need. Jesus is our counselor. He gives the best advice and knows the best choices, decisions, and plans for your life. He has walked this earth and knows exactly what you should do in every circumstance. He is not just a counselor but He is the wonderful counselor. No one can match His counsel. His word, the Bible, reveals all the details and secrets to life's questions. No appointments are necessary with this counselor. He is always available.

Christ is called "the Mighty God." Jesus is one in essence with the Father. Jesus is God. The child bearing the name "the mighty God" is, according to His divine person and divine nature, the mighty God. This title verifies His deity. Jesus, who was born in Bethlehem, is the mighty God. The word *mighty* sometimes has the connotation of being strong in battle. That is why some have translated this "warrior God." Christ fights for His people. His might is manifest everywhere in creation. He causes animals to be born. He causes the warm winds to blow. His might is evident as He transforms sinful humans who hate Him and His sovereign reign into loving sons and daughters.

Christ is "the Everlasting Father." Why is Christ called "Father"? Isn't He distinct from the first person of the holy Trinity? Yes, He is personally distinct from God the Father. But here Jesus is called Father in the sense of being the originator and creator of the universe. Just as a human father gives life through his sperm, so everything that is exists because of Jesus Christ. The apostle Paul writes about how the Son of God is the "Everlasting Father": "For by him were all things created, that are in heaven, and that are in earth, visible and invisible, whether they be thrones, or dominions, or principalities, or powers: all things were created by him, and for him: and he is before all things, and by him all things consist" (Colossians 1:16–17). There never was a time when the Son of God did not exist. He is before all things. He is the eternally begotten Son, the eternal Creator.

Christ is "the Prince of Peace." His reign is one of peace: limitless, boundless peace. Peace is a harmony that exists because there has been reconciliation between former enemies. The sin of us humans involves us declaring war on God. By nature we are enemies of God who are deserving of His righteous judgments. Jesus has reconciled His people with the Father. By faith in Jesus Christ we have peace with God. Peace flows from Jesus. He not only gives peace but is Peace. Paul loved to call God "the God of peace." Timothy speaks about it this way, "Grace, mercy and peace from God the Father and Christ Jesus our Lord" (I Timothy 1:2).

These lyrics in the Messiah celebrate the awesome titles of the Christ. These titles reveal His glorious deity. They also communicate that He is the Prince of peace. He is our Warrior God.

Thinking It Over

1.   When was the last time you used God's Word to provide you with wise counsel?

2. What does it mean that Jesus is "Wonderful Counselor"?

3. How can Jesus be called the "Everlasting Father"?

4. If your master is the "Prince of Peace," how should this effect the way you deal with conflict?

Pastoral Symphony

The title that Handel gives to the next piece, "Pastoral Symphony," portrays the idea of a peaceful sheepfold. The music of the orchestra depicts an idyllic countryside. Handel is preparing us for the next scene, which involves "shepherds abiding in the field." But he first puts us into the sandals of the shepherds who were calmly watching their sheep at night before the angels appeared.

As the "Pastoral Symphony" plays, we imagine the colors of a sunset. We hear birds tweeting their evening songs. We envision sheep with filled bellies lying down around the shepherds. We hear crickets and toads by a gurgling stream. In the wide expanse of the countryside, the solitary evening star beams. Darkness falls, and thousands of stars and constellations appear.

Shepherds quietly talk as they stoke a fire to keep warm. Are a couple of the older shepherds nodding off? Does a married shepherd lay a lamb across his lap as he thinks of his wife and little ones at home?

While the title "Prince of Peace" still rings in our ears, we are given time to contemplate the peace that we enjoy as Christ's sheep. We are safe and well fed. Peace is a calmness of spirit, with no worries or fears—just contentment. Although God may send sickness or difficulties, we can peacefully rest in His sovereignty over all things. Those who keep their eyes on the Savior enjoy peace.

A remnant in Israel faithfully watched and waited for the arrival of the Prince of Peace. People were traveling to cities in which they were born to pay the taxes imposed on them. Did they ponder the Old Testament prophesy, "But thou, Bethlehem Ephratah, though thou be little among the thousands of Judah, yet out of thee shall he come forth unto me that is to be ruler in Israel; whose goings forth have been from of old, from everlasting" (Micah 5:2).

Mothers opened their homes to family and friends. Did they approach their work with thoughts of the One who would turn their spirit of heaviness into a garment of praise? After a busy day, did the farmers rest, yearning for the One who would judge the poor with righteousness? After hours of play, did the children lay near their parents wondering who would come to rescue Israel? Earlier, the Bethlehem market had boomed with busyness. Now the dusty feet that had walked the streets needed to be washed before their owners crawled into bed. A remnant waited.

The little town of Bethlehem went to sleep unaware that God would come to the countryside of Bethlehem with a magnificent nighttime visit.

It is striking that God sends the first birth announcement of the Messiah to shepherds. He certainly is accenting that Christ would "feed his flock like a shepherd . . . gather the lambs with his arm, and carry them in his bosom, and . . . gently lead those that are with young" (Isaiah 40:11).

By Jesus's time shepherds had a bad reputation. They were viewed as thieves. If someone couldn't get a better job, he was a shepherd. Shepherds couldn't testify in a court of law. And yet when Messiah was born, God sent the first birth announcement to lowly shepherds. He was signaling that the Shepherd King was born. God also emphasized that in His decree of election He chooses many who are poor and unknown so that no one would glory in His presence.

Jesus will come again. In His first coming He sacrificed Himself for His people. At His second coming He will deliver His people and judge the wicked. No one seemed to notice Jesus's first coming—except for a few shepherds. The people in Bethlehem went on with their busy lives. The Bible says that it will be the same at the end. Just like in the days of Noah when the wicked world went on in their ungodly ways until they were suddenly destroyed by the cataclysm of the flood, so in the last days the wicked will continue on with their lives until they are surprised by the second coming of Jesus.

Jesus wants us to wait and watch for His second coming. We are to be like the wise virgins who watched for the bridegroom, anticipating his return. Jesus commands, "Watch therefore, for ye know neither the day nor the hour wherein the Son of man cometh" (Matthew 25:13).

The aged widow Anna is a model to imitate. She "departed not from the temple, but served God with fastings and prayers night and day" (Luke 2:37). Jesus says, "Watch therefore: for ye know not what hour your Lord doth come" (Matthew 24:42).

The people in Bethlehem were caught off guard by the appearance of the Christ. Do not be caught off guard at the second coming. If Jesus is precious to you, then you will anticipate His return.

If we are honest with ourselves, we often anticipate a hot cup of coffee or tea more than Jesus's second coming. When are cold and wet, we want a hot shower. When we are hungry, we can only think of our next meal. We have trained our minds to respond to basic needs. We need to train ourselves to prepare for our Savior's return.

Thinking It Over

1. How should your life be affected by the fact that your bridegroom will soon return on the clouds of heaven?

2. Describe the scene that Handel tries to portray in his "Pastoral Symphony."

3. Why did God send a birth announcement to lowly shepherds?

There Were Shepherds Abiding

And there were in the same country shepherds abiding in the field, keeping watch over their flock by night. And, lo, the angel of the Lord came upon them, and the glory of the Lord shone round about them: and they were sore afraid.
—Luke 2:8–9

The soprano soloist sings, "There were shepherds abiding in the field, keeping watch over their flock by night" (Luke 2:8), in a recitative fashion with minimal accompaniment. Her solo continues over four measures. It changes the mood. It helps the listener to recalibrate to the scene of the countryside outside Bethelehem. These words lead into the excitement found in the following verse (in Luke 2:9) that celebrates the arrival of a messenger angel.

In the countryside around Bethlehem shepherds were tending to their flocks of sheep. Their job was to ensure that the sheep had plenty of fresh grass and water. When the hot Bethlehem sun sank below the horizon it became cool and the shepherds might have needed to build a bonfire for warmth. It might sound romantic to be a shepherd, but their job was a 24/7 occupation that continued into the night as they warded off night prowlers. Sleeping sheep would make easy meals for sly wolves. Shepherds must be constantly on watch.

But!

> Their regular shepherd duty is interrupted.
> Their peaceful, quieted hearts are alarmed.
> Poise is overcome with fear.
> Into the shepherd's world descends an angel.
> Bursting into the darkness comes the glory of the Lord.
> Silence is broken with good news!
> To the people agonizing in sin comes great joy!
> Suddenly into this pastoral scene enters a praising host.
> They offer worship and adoration to God in the highest and
> blessings of peace and goodwill toward men.

Visits by angels in the Old Testament were uncommon. Such rare visits happened at unique times in redemptive history. The four hundred intertestamental years (between Malachi and Matthew) had been a time of silence. God had not spoken by prophets or communicated by angelic visitors. Then four angel visits happened over a short period. This is because we are at a turning point in redemptive history. The Messiah was coming into the world. Mary, Joseph, and Zachariah received angel visits. But the visit to the shepherds was the first to a large gathering. The shepherds were selected for a visit as representatives of the despised people of God in this world.

The shepherds tried to process the visit of a mighty angel. They were terrified. I imagine that their fear was like that of a child who is caught in the act of doing something wrong. The shepherds probably weren't very pious. Perhaps they shuddered in fear because of their sinfulness. They received a glimpse of heavenly perfection and glory. Quickly the attention was focused away from them. This visit was not about their sins. It was not a visitation in judgment. It was the birth announcement of the One who was the only hope for sinful shepherds. The angel came with good news!

The shepherds tasted the goodness of God. They saw a display of God's magnificent splendor. They not only saw a shining angel but the glory of the Lord shone around them: "And the glory of the Lord shone round about them; and they were sore afraid." God was present, appearing in His shekinah glory. And He sent a glorious, shining angel. The angel had come from the presence of the eternal God, shimmering with reflective glory. Just as the moon does not shine of itself but reflects the glory of the sun, so this angel shone because he was fresh from the presence of the God who is light. God had sent the angel on a mission.

Hundreds of years before, Moses had asked to see God's glory: "I beseech thee, shew me thy glory" (Exodus 33:18). "And the LORD said, Behold, there is a place by me, and thou shalt stand upon a rock: and it shall come to pass, while my glory passeth by, that I will put thee in a clift of the rock, and will cover thee with my hand while I pass by: and I will take away mine hand, and thou shalt see my back parts: but my face shall not be seen" (Exodus 33:21–23). Moses saw the goodness of God pass before him.

And now some unknown shepherds see the glory of the Lord and are addressed by a mighty angel.

Thinking It Over

1. We live in a day when fear is gone. People have a hard time even blushing over sin. Why is this?

2. Should we expect to receive angel visits today? Why or why not?

3. What does it mean to fear God, and why should you fear Him?

4. How should you imitate holy angels?

5. Why is it important that we not only meditate on the holiness of God but also on His goodness?

And the Angel Said unto Them

And the angel said unto them, Fear not: for, behold, I bring you good tidings of great joy, which shall be to all people. For unto you is born this day in the city of David a Saviour, which is Christ the Lord.
—Luke 2:10–11

The clear voice of the soprano soloist repeats the angel's announcement to the shepherds. Handel uses a soprano solo to mimic the angel, who bids the shepherds not to fear.

The shepherds we meet in Luke 2 were guarding sheep outside the city of Bethlehem. Sheep were an important part of the ancient economy. People ate mutton and sheared the sheep for wool. Sheep were necessary for sacrifices and offerings in the temple. But shepherds were looked down on by their fellow countrymen. Being a shepherd was considered a job for the down and out.

The night was dark; peace and quiet had settled in as the animals huddled nearby. A bonfire had been built to keep the shepherds warm, and perhaps a shepherd plucked his harp, singing a psalm of David. Into this peaceful, pastoral scene descended an angel. This was such an unexpected event! The shepherds' immediate response was fear: "They were sore afraid" (Luke 2:9). An extreme case of fear quickly overcame their peaceful situation! Not only had a shining angel appeared into the dark night but "the glory of the Lord shone round about them" (Luke 2:9).

The angel of the Lord had just come from the presence of the Lord of Hosts. The angel radiated with the glory of God. This glow was probably much like the one Moses had after he had been in the presence of God on the mountain. God is so holy that when an angel comes into God's presence, glorious holiness radiates into the darkness around him. As they met this heavenly visitor and came face-to-face with God's glory, the shepherds would have immediately been struck with God's purity and holiness and their own ungodliness.

This morning I took off plastic that had been around our windows during the winter. The windows seemed to be clean until the afternoon sun hit that side of the house. It is amazing what the sun can reveal! The shepherds must have found themselves in a situation like this when God's glory was revealed. In the presence of God's glory and purity their own sinfulness must have stood out.

God was keenly aware of the fears the shepherds felt. He sent His angel to quiet them with the words "Fear not." You might wonder why they were told not to fear. Shouldn't sinful men be afraid of a holy God and His messengers? Yes, we are guilty, but that is not the whole story.

> Who? ········ Christ the Lord
>
> What? ········ a Savior
>
> Occasion? ········ is born
>
> When? ········ this day
>
> Where? ········ in the city of David
>
> Why? ········ for you

The shepherds, who were considered by others to be untrustworthy, were entrusted by God with "good tidings of great joy" (Luke 2:10). They received the most amazing message—a happy message that gives hope and joy. It is a message for the old and for the young; for the rich and the poor alike; for the strong and weak; and for people of every color, tribe, and nationality. The angel came with all the information. He announced a birth and told the shepherds who was born, where the baby was located, and what the baby was born to do.

Since every human is a sinner and every sin is against God, we need a Savior. Paul writes,

> There is none righteous, no, not one: There is none that understandeth, There is none that seeketh after God. They are all gone out of the way, they are together become unprofitable; there is none that doeth good, no, not one (Romans 3:10–12).

Only God can take away sin. He has given us a Savior, Jesus Christ, who is one in being with the Father. Jesus is God, and He saves. The message of the angel is good news because the Savior has come to save His people.

The shepherds leave their sheep to visit the city of David. They find a babe wrapped in swaddling clothes and lying in a manger, just as the angel had said.

Thinking It Over

1.   What sins make you fearful of facing God?

2. What does it mean that God has justified you?

3. How do you experience the truth of your justification?

4. As justified Christians, why do we not need to fear Judgment Day?

Suddenly There Was with the Angel

And suddenly there was with the angel
a multitude of the heavenly host praising God.
—Luke 2:13

Now the soprano recitative moves at a brisker tempo as a multitude of angels appear in the countryside. The rhythm and the text paint the portrait of the sudden arrival of the angel army from the glories of heaven to a field outside the little town of Bethlehem where shepherds were keeping watch over their flocks. First, just one angel appeared to the shepherds. The angel tried to take away the shepherds' fear. The next moment, an angel army arrived; the sky was filled with the heavenly host.

A huge number of angels assembled, praising God. Praise involves celebrating someone's glorious attributes or works. Synonyms of the word *praise* are glorify, bless, extol, honor, worship, and adoration. The heavenly host broke forth in praise to God.

- Praise befits the King!

> Great is the LORD, and greatly to be praised in the city of our God, in the mountain of his holiness (Psalm 48:1).

- Praise verbalizes the goodness of God.
    For his merciful kindness is great toward us: and the truth of the LORD endureth forever. Praise ye the LORD (Psalm 117:2).

    I will extol thee, my God, O king; and I will bless thy name for ever and ever (Psalm 145:1).

- Criticism destroys praise.

    They forgot God their saviour, which had done great things in Egypt . . . but murmured in their tents, and hearkened not unto the voice of the LORD (Psalm 106:21, 25).

    Do all things without murmuring and disputings (Philippians 2:14).

- God is infinite, and His praise is immeasurable.
    I will praise thee, O Lord my God, with all my heart: and I will glorify thy name for evermore (Psalm 86:12).

- Everything that breathes has been commanded to praise the Lord.

    Let everything that hath breath praise the LORD. Praise ye the LORD (Psalm 150:6).
    O praise the LORD, all ye nations: praise him, all ye people (Psalm 117:1).

- Praise is to arise every day.
    Every day will I bless thee; and I will praise thy name for ever and ever (Psalm 145:2).

It is a good thing to give thanks unto the LORD, and to sing praises unto thy name, O Most High: to shew forth thy lovingkindness in the morning, and thy faithfulness every night (Psalm 92:1–2).

- Worship includes praise.

Give unto the LORD the glory due unto his name; worship the LORD in the beauty of holiness (Psalm 29:2).

Exalt ye the LORD our God, and worship at his footstool; for he is holy (Psalm 99:5).

- Praise is expressed in song.

Let the saints be joyful in glory: let them sing aloud upon their beds. Let the high praises of God be in their mouth (Psalm 149:5–6).

Oh sing unto the LORD a new song; for he hath done marvellous things: his right hand, and his holy arm, have gotten him the victory (Psalm 98:1).

- Prayer includes praise.

Wherefore David blessed the LORD before all the congregation: and David said, Blessed be thou, LORD God of Israel our father, for ever and ever. Thine, O LORD, is the greatness, and the power, and the glory, and the victory, and the majesty: for all that is in the heaven and in the earth is thine; thine is the kingdom,

O LORD, and thou art exalted as head above all (1 Chronicles 29:10–11).

Praise is a verb and must be an action. Our hearts must be engaged in the activity of praise. Without our hearts being affected, our praise is merely empty words.

Thinking It Over

1. Are you murmuring and complaining, or are you praising God? Explain.

2. What is your favorite song of praise?

3. Write a prayer of praise to God.

Glory to God

Glory to God in the highest, and on earth peace, goodwill toward men
(Luke 2:14).

Handel begins this chorus about the glory of God with a high F#. Handel is highlighting of God is far exalted above us. That is why the music goes so high as the choir sings: "Glory to God in the highest." He contrasts these words sung with high notes with the low notes sung by the tenor and bass when they say the words "and peace on earth." A great gap exists between men on earth and our exalted God.

We can listen in on what the shepherds heard. A host of heavenly angels burst forth with praise to God. A great multitude of angels sang: "Glory to God in the highest, and on earth peace, goodwill toward men."

These angels constantly gaze upon God in His glory and majesty. He is exalted high in Paradise. His great work of salvation is something that they "desire to look into" (I Peter 1:12). They marveled over the peace He brings to men who were apart from Him. Now they share the good news on earth.

The Westminster Shorter Confession asked the question, "What is the chief end of man?" It answers with the words "a man's chief end is to glorify God and to enjoy him forever." This must be the whole focus of life! We were formed and reformed to glorify God. Our chief purpose must be to bring honor to the King of kings.

What is glory? Glory is the display of the inherent holiness of God: "And when all the children of Israel saw how the fire came down, and the glory of the Lord upon the house, they bowed themselves with their faces to the ground upon the pavement, and worshiped, and praise the Lord, saying, for he is good; for his mercy and to earth forever" (2 Chronicles 7:3). !Glory is a brilliant and illuminating revelation of the hidden attributes of God. When God's glory is witnessed, His people will be moved to:

- **Love Him.** "Thou shalt love the Lord thy God with all thy heart, and with all thy soul, and with all thy strength, and with all thy mind; and thy neighbor as thyself" (Luke 10:27).

- **Obey Him**. "If ye love me, keep my commandments" (John 14:15).

- **Thank Him.** "It is a good thing to give thanks unto the Lord, and to sing praises unto thy name, O most high" (Psalm 92:1).

- **Bless Him in song.** "Bless the Lord, O my soul; and all that is within me, bless his holy name" (Psalm 103:1).

- **Seek Him in prayer.** "Seek ye the Lord while he may be found, call ye upon him while he is near" (Isaiah 55:6).

- **Know Him through His word.** Read the Bible. "Blessed is the man . . . (whose) delight is in the law of the Lord; and in his law doth he meditate day and night" (Psalm 1:1–2).

- **Confess your sins against Him.** "He that cover of his sins shall not prosper: but whoso confesses and for sake of them shall have mercy" (Proverbs 28:13).

The opposite of glorifying God is to belittle, criticize and dishonor Him. We do this when we make idols of the things of this world. Do you have an addiction? It is your idol?

One way we dishonor God is by being thankless. How often we go to the grocery store and get all the things we need to put them away in the house without ever thanking the Lord for His provisions. We belittle God when we do not read His Word, speak to Him in prayer, or sing to Him.

Handel creatively takes the glorious message that is so high and lofty down to planet earth as the chorus sings slowly and meditatively "and peace on earth." Peace flows from this glorious God towards men of His good pleasure. The translation of the King James version is not the best. It reads "peace on earth, *goodwill toward men.*" This might imply universalism—as if Jesus came to save all human beings. But that is not a good translation. A better translation is "men of His good pleasure." The reference to God's good pleasure is a reference to sovereign election. Why has God chosen you? The Apostle Paul tells us that God has chosen us out of His sovereign good pleasure. Our election was unconditional. Christ has come to reveal God's good pleasure towards elect humanity.

After these last peaceful words are sung, the orchestra fades away much like the angels quietly disappearing from the shepherd's sight.

Thinking It Over

   1.   What is the glory of God?

2. What do the angels mean by "goodwill toward men"? Why isn't this the best translation of the original text?

3. Compare a life lived for one's own glory and living for the glory of God.

4. Which of the seven, aspects of a life focused on Christ above, needs the most attention in your life? How will plan to grow in this area?

5. What is the peace of God's good pleasure?

Rejoice Greatly, O Daughter of Zion

*Rejoice greatly, O daughter of Zion; shout, O daughter of Jerusalem:
behold, thy King cometh unto thee . . . and he shall speak peace unto
the heathen
.—Zechariah 9:9–10*

The daughters of Jerusalem and Zion are commanded to rejoice. These daughters are the offspring of Jerusalem, the children of the church. Old and young, men and women, infants and children alike are to celebrate the arrival of the King. The descendants of the church of Christ who know Him personally are to raise an exuberant sound.

Likewise, you are to release your enthusiasm in a shout of exultation. There is to be no holding back. No excuses like "I just keep my emotions inside" are allowed. No! You have been charged to delight in your King. People who delight in fine wine express their joy in it. When a fan of a major league baseball team sees his favorite star hit a home run, he rejoices. When the person you wanted to be elected as president is installed into office, you rejoice.

We must rejoice in the messianic King.

Our King has come! Rejoice greatly! This is not a quiet joy. This is supersized rejoicing! A far-reaching shout! Is your life characterized by abundant rejoicing in Christ? Do those who encounter you detect that you have great joy? Have you placed your "joy button" on mute? Have you forgotten your purpose? Have you lost sight of the object of your joy?

What is all this gladness about? Why should the daughters of Jerusalem be so happy? Why this exuberant joy? Can you imagine the excitement if you were summoned to the Oval Office to receive a medal of honor? Our King does something even more unprecedented; He comes to us. Our King knows us. He knows where we are and the state in which He will find us. And He humbled Himself to come to us.

Zechariah 9 reveals the nature of our King, detailing these qualities:	
Our King is *"just"* (v. 9).	Our King is just and therefore must punish all sin. He takes on Himself the sin of the elect and gives us His righteousness.
Our King is *"lowly"* (v. 9).	Our King is humble. He does not ride on a kingly horse but on a colt. He is a Servant King, leading by serving.
Our King *"speak[s] peace unto the heathen"* (v. 10).	God no longer looks at us as enemies because our King has taken our sin on Himself. He speaks peace to those who once were enemies.
Our King's *"dominion shall be from sea even to sea"* (v. 10).	This King's dominion reaches from the Atlantic Ocean to the Pacific Ocean, and from the bodies of water in the south to those above the North Sea.

Our King *"shall save them as the flock of his people"* (v. 16).	Our King is a shepherd who tends the needs of His flock. He leads us in green pastures and protects us from evil.
From our King flows *"goodness"* (v. 17)	Our King is pure and does only what is good.
Our King's *"beauty"* is great! (v. 17)	Our King is beautiful in all His glorious attributes. Like the facets of a sparkling diamond, His glory and beauty shine forth.

This is our King! He rules over us, and we are His rejoicing citizens! What affection He has for His subjects. His law is our delight, and under His rule we prosper.

Ancient prophecy said that the messianic King would speak peace to the Gentiles. He speaks peace to the heathen! Whoever would have thought this possible? This is the unimaginable and unexpected reason to rejoice. Isn't salvation limited to the Jews, the physical descendants of Abraham? But God sends His Son into the world to gather a holy catholic church out of the nations of the world.

It seems as if the words *peace* and *heathen* do not belong in the same sentence. Yet God has chosen to show mercy to Gentile idolaters. Christ's kingdom extends to elect Gentiles throughout all the nations of the world. It was prophesied that "He shall have dominion also from sea to sea, and from the river unto the ends of the earth" (Psalm 72:8). Christ has spoken peace to many Gentiles. If you are a Gentile who has heard this word of peace and forgiveness from Jesus, you have reason to sing hallelujah!

Thinking It Over

1. In your ordinary, daily life, what do you get happy about?

2. Who are the daughters of Zion?

3. Why should you rejoice in King Jesus?

4. What does it mean that the Messiah will "speak peace to the heathen"?

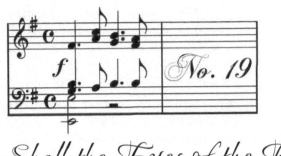

Then Shall the Eyes of the Blind

Then the eyes of the blind shall be opened, and the ears of the deaf shall be
unstopped. Then shall the lame man leap as an hart,
and the tongue of the dumb sing.
—Isaiah 35:5–6

Recitative 19 was written for the alto soloist. It is so brief that the listener scarcely has time to process the astonishing events that are mentioned. The words are "sung-spoken," and great emphasis is placed on strong, even shocking words like "opened," "unstopped," "leap," and "sing."

Perhaps you found your mind leaping from this ancient prophecy to the ministry of Jesus when He miraculously healed many people who were blind, deaf, lame, and dumb. Isaiah 35:5–6 presents us with four astounding miracles that should take our breath away. Jesus miraculously healed Jews with these physical ailments. He healed the blind, deaf, lame, and dumb.

The four types of physical sicknesses that Jesus healed are pictures of spiritual sicknesses. Jesus's miracles were not just displays of omnipotent power. They were signs. The healing of physical ailments pointed to spiritual realities.

The Blind Shall See

John 9 records the wonderful story of the man who was blind from birth. Jesus "spat on the ground, and made clay of the spittle, and he anointed the eyes of the blind man with the clay, and said unto him, Go, wash in the pool of Siloam, (which is by interpretation, Sent.) He went his way therefore, and washed, and came seeing" (vv. 6–7). This was a life-changing miracle! People who are born blind normally do not end up seeing. The blind man testifies that since the creation of the world this had never happened before (v. 32).

The spiritual eyes of a person must be opened for him or her to see Christ. Just as people who are born blind do not see unless God heals, a person, apart from the work of the Holy Spirit, cannot believe in Jesus Christ. To believe in Jesus Christ as the Son of God and only Savior requires spiritual eyesight. This sight is even more miraculous than seeing with one's physical eyes. Do you have spiritual eyes that see Christ in His glory?

The Deaf Shall Hear

Mark 7:31–37 records the story of Jesus healing a man who was deaf in the region of Decapolis. Since hearing and speech are so interrelated, this deaf man could not talk. The people begged Jesus to heal the man. Jesus "put his finger into his ears, and he spit, and touched his tongue; and looking up to heaven, he sighed, and saith unto him, Ephphatha, that is, Be opened. And straightway his ears were opened, and the string of his tongue was loosed, and he spake plain" (vv. 33–35). Without looking at the man's medical records and researching what part of the ear was not properly functioning, Jesus merely says "Be opened." And the man can hear. He didn't need years of speech therapy. He spoke plainly.

Our ears must be unstopped in order to hear Christ speak through His word. No man, apart from the work of the Holy Spirit, can hear the Good Shepherd calling. Since the fall of Adam and Eve, all men have stopped-up ears. Paul writes about this in 1 Corinthians 2:14: "But the natural man receiveth not the things of the Spirit of God: for they are foolishness unto him: neither can he know them, because they are spiritually discerned." Have your spiritual ears been opened?

The Lame Shall Walk

In John 5 we meet an invalid who has lain on his bed for thirty-eight years. It was even more difficult to be lame in the days before wheelchairs. Jesus says to the lame man, "Rise, take up thy bed, and walk" (v. 8). At once the man was healed, and he took up his bed and walked. Imagine the running and leaping that took place on that day!

Men and women who will not follow Christ or be His disciples are spiritually lame. They are pictured in John 6:66: "From that time many of his disciples went back, and walked no more with him." But those who deny themselves, take up their cross, and follow Jesus are no longer lame. Are you following Jesus?

The Dumb Shall Sing

When I read about the dumb singing, I think of Zechariah, the priest who disbelieved the message of the angel Gabriel and was made mute. For nine months he could not speak. Imagine how hard it must have been to keep quiet about the story of Gabriel's visit and his excitement over his elderly wife's pregnancy. On the day when Zechariah was naming his newly born son John, there was a question about what to name the baby. The elderly priest wrote on a tablet, "His name is John."

And the mute spoke: "And his mouth was opened immediately, and his tongue loosed, and he spake, and praised God" (Luke 1:64). Zechariah was then filled with the Holy Spirit and confessed that God had raised up a horn of salvation and his son, John, would prepare the way for the Messiah (vv. 68–79). Has your tongue been loosed to speak about what God in Christ has done for you?

Thinking It Over

1. What is a biblical miracle?

2. How are you by nature blind? Even as a Christian, what blind spots exist in your spiritual sight?

3. How is your spiritual hearing? How do you listen to sermons?

4. Why did Jesus heal lame people? What spiritual reality does this particular miraculous sign point to in your life?

5. To what extent is your mouth still mute?

He Shall Feed His Flock

He shall feed his flock like a shepherd: he shall gather the lambs with his arm, and carry them in his bosom, and shall gently lead those that are with young.
—Isaiah 40:11

Come unto me, all ye that labour and are heavy laden, and I will give you rest. Take my yoke upon you, and learn of me; for I am meek and lowly in heart: and ye shall find rest unto your souls.
—Matthew 11:28–29

Have you ever watched sheep graze? Handel reflects the slow grazing habits of sheep, choosing the appropriate tempo to fit the words of this text. I tried singing the solo more quickly, and it ruined the mood and took away the gentle, restful impression that Handel's music gives. The text and words fit together nicely.

Isaiah provides a beautiful description of the Savior as a shepherd. David uses this metaphor in Psalm 23:1 where he sings, "The Lord is my shepherd." Jesus continues to use this metaphor in the New Testament. He says, "I am the Good Shepherd" (John 10:11). God cares for His church as a shepherd cares for his flock. God lives among us and sees that we are fed by His word. He not only gives us the Bible so that we can know Him and read about His love but He gives us preachers to teach us, much like a shepherd leads his sheep to green pastures where they can graze.

A good shepherd sacrificially tends to the needs of his sheep. Through rain, sleet, and snow he cares for the health and protection of his animals. He protects them from lions. He rescues wandering sheep from the danger that threatens such folly. He applies medicine to sick sheep. He anoints their heads with oil to protect them from biting flies and sunburn. God has a personal interest in His flock because His elect sheep belong to Him. Christ sacrificially tends to His people. He protects us from devilish lions, and He protects His church from wolves in sheep's clothing. He applies the balm of Gilead.

Christ feeds us along lush pastures. He leads us to living streams of water. "He maketh me to lie down in green pastures: he leadeth me beside the still waters" (Psalm 23:2). Have you eaten from the green pastures of your Shepherd? Are you feeding on Him by meditating on His word?

Jesus told the parable of the lost sheep in Luke 15:1–7. After finding the lost sheep, the shepherd takes it home on his shoulders, rejoicing. Whether the lamb is lost or whether it is weak, our gentle Savior picks him up with His strong arms and carries him safely home. Christ doesn't allow us to keep wandering in sin. We are prone to wander, but Christ is prone to come and find us. Our Shepherd holds His sheep up when they are unable stand by themselves. I imagine a shepherd taking up a little lamb not many days old and cuddling it close to himself as he walks. Our Savior knows His sheep, and His sheep hear His voice (see John 10:27). There is a close bond of fellowship between Christ and us. It is like the intimate relationship between shepherds and their sheep.

Our Shepherd is gentle. "He gently leads those that are with young." He is not harsh and impatient. He does not beat the sheep with a rod or tell them to get going. He calmly and tenderly leads them. He provides them with shelter. He guides them in the way of righteousness.

This gentle Shepherd commands us, His sheep, to come to Him. This command is spoken with power. It is not a weak, ineffective command, as if the Shepherd is helplessly pleading for His sheep to come to Him. This command does not reflect some blind hope on the Good Shepherd's part that His elect sheep will approach Him in faith. No, it is a sovereign and effectual call. When Christ calls, His elect sheep do hear because He gives them ears to hear. Our Shepherd's call is the call of a king. It is one hundred percent successful. He powerfully calls and draws His sheep to Himself. They hear, and they come. In Romans 8:29–30, the apostle Paul reveals the Golden Chain of Salvation. This chain has five links. The first is God foreknowing His elect sheep. God set His love on His sheep before time began. The second link is that those on whom God has set His love He predestinates. This means that He ordains certain lost, elect sheep to be conformed to the image of Jesus. The third link is that Jesus, by His Spirit, effectually and powerfully calls elect sinners to Himself. The fourth link is that God justifies those whom He has regenerated, called, and given faith in His Son. The final link is that those whom God has foreknown, predestinated, called, and justified He also glorifies. That is, He brings them to ultimate salvation in glory.

Our Shepherd promises "soul rest" to His sheep. Christ's sheep hear His voice and they realize that they are sinners who need a Redeemer. Fleeing to Christ, the sheep find a Savior who is their justification. They find in Christ a God and Savior who is able to protect them.

Thinking It Over

1. What are the greatest challenges of being a shepherd?

2. How do earthly shepherds fall short of what Christ is like as the Good Shepherd?

3. What does it mean that the Good Shepherd is "gentle"? How does He manifest this gentleness?

4. What does the psalmist mean when he says that God's "gentleness hath made me great"? (See Psalm 18:35)

His Yoke Is Easy

For my yoke is easy, and my burden is light.
—Matthew 11:30

A yoke crafted from solid wood can be heavy. Any burden that you carry around for a while can become burdensome.

It amuses me that Handel composes music that is light and airy about yokes and burdens. He brilliantly creates music that soars. He communicates the idea that the Messiah conveyed when He said, "My yoke is easy, and my burden is light."

Jesus was in the cornfield on the Sabbath day with His disciples. Being hungry, they plucked some wheat to eat. The Pharisees saw this and were enraged at this unlawful activity on the Sabbath day. They had invented six hundred oral traditions, which were human commandments.

The Pharisees did not think that they needed a Messiah to save them from their sins. They imagined that they could obtain heaven by law keeping. They had come to believe that people's obedience was at least a partial basis for their salvation. In other words, the way to heaven was by keeping the divine law and following the traditions of the elders.

Jesus calls out, "Come to Me." Jesus announces that salvation is found in Him. The law of God is a yoke that was too heavy for the Jews to bear. The traditions of the elders were a heavy burden on legalists. Coming to Jesus is an act of faith. Those who come to Jesus believe two things: first, they believe that Jesus has kept the law perfectly on their behalf; second, they believe that Jesus has paid the penalty for the sins of His people. Jesus says, "All that the Father giveth me shall come to me; and him that cometh to me I will in no wise cast out" (John 6:37).

Jesus calls the laboring and heavy laden to Himself. He does not have in mind the hard-working labor that results in sore muscles. He is calling those who are burdened by their sin. He is calling those who are heavy laden by the legalistic traditions of men. Are you troubled over your sin? Do you seek peace and calm for your soul? Do you know that you need God's help to deal with your guilt? Then you are among those who labor and are heavy laden. Jesus calls to Himself such helpless sinners who know they need Christ.

Those who are heavy laden find their sin to be a burden. They hate their sins and how their guilt places a barrier between them and God. They feel the heavy weight of sin and all the troubles that accrue from evil.

Jesus tells such people who are "poor in spirit" to come to Him. He will give them rest. His yoke is easy and His burden is light. It is a rough business when you are a child of the Devil. The Devil does not look out for the welfare of his children. They exist to serve him. Satan uses and abuses wicked people. There is no rest for the wicked.

But Jesus gives rest. It is not a hardship to follow Jesus—such is the love and encouragement that you enjoy. Even the suffering that is involved with following Jesus is a small thing; it hardly compares to the eternal weight of glory.

Take Christ's yoke on yourself and learn from Him. Jesus uses an example of a yoke that is placed around the neck of an ox. A yoke was a fitted piece of wood that was placed around the neck of oxen or other animals as they pulled a plow. It was crafted to be smooth so that it would not rub or irritate the animal that wore it. Necks of a pair of oxen were fitted in a U-shaped cuff that attached to the wooden yoke. The oxen would need to walk together in unison as they pulled a cart or plowed a field. This would distribute the weight evenly between the animals.

Jesus says, "Take my yoke upon you." You might question why someone would want to put on a yoke. Scripture lays out two diverse yokes. The yoke of Christ is an easy yoke, a yoke of liberty and joyful submission. With Christ as our teacher, we learn that His royal law is not grievous. We can call our burdens light because we have our eyes fixed on the "eternal weight of glory" (2 Corinthians 4:17). The exalted Son of God helps us to bear our yoke.

The yoke of bondage is a yoke of slavery. This is the bondage Martin Luther knew as an unconverted monk. He could not find rest. He confessed his sins for hours and woke up in the middle of the night to pray and sing. He crawled up the steps of a church in Rome to get dead people released from purgatory. He wore a prickly hair shirt. He labored as a monk, and the yoke was heavy.

Luther thought that salvation could be earned by obeying the "do this" and "don't do this" of the law.

Don't think, *If I am careful enough, I will be saved. If I show up at church two times on Sunday, wear a suit or my best dress, and oblige my parents, then I'm in.* No. Confess your sins and look to Jesus for righteousness.

In contrast to proud sinners who imagine that by their own good works they are racking up points with God, Jesus says, "Come to Me." You can't get the burden of sin off your back by law keeping. Instead, you need to flee to Jesus, who alone can take away your guilt.

Don't go to the Pharisees, who will simply give you a heavier yoke to bear. They will always be inventing new traditions and requiring new obedience to human commandments. They will not lighten your burden. Don't go to alcohol or drugs with your burden. Your burden will not be lightened. You will wake up with a hangover or in a jail cell.

Flee to Jesus with the burden of your guilt and sin, and He will bear it away. He will give you a new yoke—a light one. Seeking first Christ's kingdom will involve untold joy.

Thinking It Over

1. What is a yoke?

2. What heavy yoke did the Pharisees place on the Jews?

3. How does Jesus take away your burden?

4. Why is the burden of being a disciple of Jesus only a light burden?

Messiah

Part 2

The Accomplishment of Redemption by the Sacrifice of Jesus, Man's Rejection of God's Offer, and Mankind's utter Defeat When Trying to Oppose the Power of the Almighty

Behold the Lamb of God

Behold the Lamb of God, which taketh away the sin of the world.
—John 1:29

All day long we look at many things. The word *behold* is an archaism that we do not use much in ordinary conversations. We tell our children to look at things. We say, "Look at that!" We tell children to look at the fireworks. We tell our loved ones to look at how bright the moon is. "Look at that baby!" we say.

John the Baptist told his contemporaries to look at someone. He said, "Behold!" He wanted to turn the eyes of his disciples toward the Messiah.

Our gaze must remain on the Messiah who takes away the sin of the world. We need to live by faith. When we fall into sin, we must look to the Lamb of God, who takes away our sins.

John the Baptist was living in the wilderness beyond the Jordan. Just days before, he had baptized the One whose sandal he was not worthy to loosen.

Now John sees Jesus approaching, and he exclaims, "Behold! The Lamb of God who takes away the sin of the world!" He knew that Jesus was the Messiah because God had revealed to him that the One on whom he would "see the Spirit descending, and remaining on him, this is he who baptizes with the Holy Ghost" (John 1:33).

John calls out, "Behold!" He tells those gathered about him in the wilderness to look and to take notice. They must ponder the amazing truth that the man walking toward them is the long-awaited Messiah.

Jesus is a young man who is only thirty years old. He is the Lamb of God, pure, spotless, and innocent. All the sacrifices of the Old Testament had pointed ahead to this Lamb of God. He has been sent by the God the Father to earth to crush the head of the serpent and to rescue His chosen saints.

It is important to observe that there is not more than one lamb. The verse does not read, "Behold the lambs of God." There are not many messiahs. There are not many saviors. There is no savior other than Jesus. We live in a world in which religious pluralism is popular. People say that salvation is found by following any god of your choice. Jesus's name is revered alongside Allah and Buddha. It is said that Jesus is just one of the possible ways back to God. But Jesus said, "I am the way, the truth, and the life: no man cometh unto the Father, but by me" (John 14:6). To believe in Jesus is to believe that He is the exclusive Lamb of God.

Jesus is the Lamb of God, God's only begotten Son in human flesh. The man Jesus is holy and pure. Jesus is pictured as a white lamb. The Bible says about the holy Lamb of God, "[He] did no sin, neither was guile found in his mouth: who, when he was reviled, reviled not again; when he suffered, he threatened not" (1 Peter 2:22–23).

In the Old Testament, God commanded that a lamb be sacrificed every morning and evening at the temple. He intended that these sacrifices would point His people to the future Messiah.

All we like sheep have gone astray (Isaiah 53:6). Our sin separates us from God. We are unholy. But the Lamb of God came to take away the sin of His people. The apostle Peter says about the Messiah: "Who his own self bare our sins in his own body on the tree, that we, being dead to sins, should live unto righteousness: by whose stripes ye were healed" (1 Peter 2:24).

John uses the broad language of the "world" to describe whose sins Jesus would take away. John the Baptist is not saying that Jesus takes away the sins of every human being born into the world. He uses this universalistic language to make the point that Jesus will save a catholic church composed of both Jews and Gentiles.

The message of John the Baptist that Jesus is the "Lamb of God who takes away the sin of the world" is a presentation of the gospel in a nutshell. In these last days, we need to behold Jesus as the Lamb of God. There is a look that saves. It is the look of faith. Look at Jesus. Look to the Lamb of God for full forgiveness.

Thinking It Over

1. How is Jesus like a lamb?

2. What is the "world" for which the Lamb of God dies? In other words, who or what is the "world" whose sins Jesus takes away?

3. What is the significance of the word *the* in the statement
    "Behold *the* Lamb of God"? Why is it important to believe that
    Jesus is the only way of salvation?

He Was Despised

He is despised and rejected of men; a man of sorrows,
and acquainted with grief.
—Isaiah 53:3

I gave my back to the smiters, and my cheeks to them
that plucked off the hair: I hid not my face from shame and spitting.
—Isaiah 50:6

Handel chose thoughtful music to communicate the raw and distressing words of the text. The perfect and pure Lamb of God was a man of sorrows. He was despised, rejected, and acquainted with grief. The inflection used to dramatically pronounce the words *despised* (it is pronounced like *rejected*, as though it has three syllables: de-spis-ed) and *rejected* come to life through Handel's use of skips and steps that are up and down. The music shifts, and we visualize the smiting of Jesus. The music is intense and passionate. Its speed and repetition feel like strokes of the whip and plucking of hair. But Jesus did not hide from this shame. His eyes remained focused on His Father.

Have you ever suffered being despised or rejected by your friends? Over the last several months I have felt despised by a familiar friend. She ignores me. She looks past me. She will engage in bubbly conversations with everyone but me. It hurts. She alters her steps when she sees me approaching. I think that slander has led her to turn her back on me. I feel rejected. Perhaps you feel rejected by someone today. When you feel rejected you can begin to relate to the rejection that the Messiah experienced.

We do not willingly endure rejection. We are not gluttons for punishment. But the Messiah willingly came into this world to suffer rejection—and not just by one person. He came to suffer rejection by His hometown people. And the entire covenant nation rejected Him.

The Messiah personally underwent the hurt of rejection. Even his closest family members rejected Him as Messiah during His ministry. When people reject us, they often just ignore us. Jesus was rejected, but this rejection included Him being given to the smiters. The religious leaders struck Him in the face. They slapped Him. They plucked out the hair of His beard. They spit in his face.

When Jesus preached in His hometown, the people whom He had grown up with first marveled at His preaching. But their hearts were fickle. A little later the families that He had grown up with tried to murder Him by throwing Him over a cliff.

Jesus was rejected by the teachers of the law, who were supposed to sit in the seat of Moses and teach what was good and true. "The scribes which came down from Jerusalem said, he hath Beelzebub, and by the prince of the devils casteth he out devils" (Mark 3:22). The teachers of the Law dare to claim that the Son of God is the prince of the devils. Even worse, they claim that mighty miracles performed by the Spirit of God are in fact the unclean actions of a demonic spirit.

Jesus experienced rejection at the hands of Judas Iscariot (Matthew 26:49). What deceit, that Judas would betray his master with a kiss! A kiss, which is supposed to be a seal of affection, becomes the means of conveying rejection.

Jesus was publicly rejected by the Jewish people when they preferred to have released Barsabbas, a rebel and murderer, rather than the Lamb of God. He was accustomed to grief and familiar with rejection.

Being rejected, Jesus experienced public disgrace. Jesus did not reject this rejection. He might have called down a legion of angels to protect Him from rejection. But He chose the way of rejection because of His great love for His people. He did not want His elect people to be rejected by God. He was rejected by God so that we might always be accepted in the Beloved.

In *Messiah* the soloist sings the words "He was despised" in an emphatic way. The sounds of the consonants in the word *de-spis-ed*, as they are sung by the soloist, remind us of the strike of the lashes on Jesus's back.

Has anyone ever spit at you out of revulsion? When the Jewish leaders spit at Jesus, He did not hide His face from this shame and spitting. He endured rejection and public ridicule.

The last thing that we fallen humans want is rejection. Young people will do crazy and wicked things to avoid being rejected by their peers. Novice gang members will commit murder so that they can receive the privilege of full membership in the gang. We know how quickly we give in to peer pressure because we want to be accepted.

But Jesus was secure in His identity as the Lamb of God who must suffer rejection for His people. He did not recoil from rejection. He accepted it. The result is that we are accepted by God and never will be rejected.

Thinking It Over

1. How have you been rejected? By whom? Why?

2. How have you dealt with disgrace? How did you respond to public shame?

3. How did Jesus suffer rejection?

4. Why did Jesus suffer rejection and disgrace?

5. Jesus's disciples are also called to suffer. The apostle Paul writes, "Yea, and all that will live godly in Christ Jesus shall suffer persecution" (2 Timothy 3:12). How are you suffering for the gospel?

Surely He Hath Borne Our Griefs

Surely he hath borne our griefs, and carried our sorrows. . . .
But he was wounded for our transgressions, he was bruised for our iniquities:
the chastisement of our peace was upon him.
—Isaiah 53:4–5

The beautiful phrase "Surely he hath borne our griefs" is sung with confidence. "Surely" implies that without a doubt it has happened. Sin has been borne, picked up, and carried away. Much like a child who falls asleep on the couch and is carried off to bed, our sin is taken by Jesus, who carries it away. He bears away the effects of sin. He takes away the pain of our guilt over our wretched sins. Christ has carried our sorrows—so that we could live in everlasting joy.

This text in *Messiah* provides such encouragement. I should post it near my kitchen sink so that I could frequently be reminded of it. Christ carries away the sorrows and grief that I would have had to endure in the lake of fire.

In the past the Messiah has already borne our griefs and carried our sorrows. The verbs "borne" and "carried" are in the past tense. I do not need to lug the troubles of this life around on my own shoulders. Christ has carried my sorrows and has earned for me the grace to endure them. He takes my challenges and makes them His own. He is always with me to assist me in the sorrows I experience in this vale of tears.

Several months ago, we rented a U-Haul truck to move a heavy collection of rocks and minerals. Our minivan would not have been able to bear the weight. The chassis of the U-Haul truck was built to carry a greater weight than our minivan. Like the heavy truck, the almighty Son of God has taken the heavy weight of our grief on Himself. We are like the minivan; by ourselves we cannot bear the weight of our sins. We cannot bear up under the great trials God sends to us in His sovereignty. Jesus, the Son of God, is strong and the only one who can bear the payment for our transgressions.

Jesus was able to bear our griefs and sorrows because He is the only begotten Son of God in human flesh. The Son of God, according to His divinity, upheld His human nature as He carried the great weight of our guilt and sin to the cross.

Jesus carried the sorrows of His covenant people as He engaged in a ministry of healing. Matthew tells us about how Jesus fulfilled ancient prophecy: "When the even was come, they brought unto him many that were possessed with devils: and he cast out the spirits with his word, and healed all that were sick: that it might be fulfilled which was spoken by Esaias the prophet, saying, Himself took our infirmities, and bare our sicknesses" (Matthew 8:16–17).

We experience so many infirmities and sicknesses in this fallen world. We catch the flu, suffer the pain of sore throats, and have high fevers. We know people who have suffered the pain of breaking a bone or the anguish of having cancer.

But griefs and sorrows are not limited to physical ailments. Worse than physical ailments can be psychological pain. What deep grief saints can suffer because of past abuse! Such sorrow is often lodged deep within the soul.

Jesus was literally wounded for our transgressions. He had physical wounds on His head from the crown of thorns being thrust on Him and from the terrible whipping He had endured. He had wounds from being struck in the face. He had wounds in His hands and His feet from the nails driven through them. "He was wounded for our transgressions." He who had never personally transgressed His Father's perfect law was wounded for our transgressions.

The Messiah was literally bruised for our iniquities. He had black-and-blue spots on His face and body. Bruises are sore to the touch. They are caused by blood vessels bursting so that blood gathers around the injured area. Jesus was a sight. Why was He bruised? He suffered these physical injuries in order to pay for the guilt of our sins, or what the sacred writer calls our "iniquities."

The chastisement for our peace was laid on the Messiah. Jesus took the Father's chastisement for our sin. God's anger for our iniquities was laid on Jesus. Chastisement is discipline applied in love. Jesus underwent this chastisement of the Father for us and suffered in our place as an act of substitutionary atonement.

Jesus Christ gives peace to those purchased by His blood. Hurricanes are deadly. They can tear apart entire cities. Even though a hurricane can cause enormous damage, at the eye of the hurricane there is stillness and peace. The result of Jesus being wounded for us is that we enjoy peace with God. Christ suffers the hurricane of the divine fury so that we might enjoy the peace and stillness found in the eye of the storm. But for us there is no storm—only the smiling countenance of a gracious God.

We are heirs of the blessed shalom that we will experience in the life to come.

Thinking It Over

1. What is the significance of the word *surely* in the text?

2. How did Jesus bear your griefs?

3. How does Jesus continue to bear your sorrows?

4. Why should we emphasize that Jesus was physically wounded and bruised?

5. What does it mean that the "chastisement for our peace" was laid on Jesus?

And with His Stripes We Are Healed

And with his stripes we are healed.
—Isaiah 53:5

It is remarkable that such solemn words can be sung with such exuberance! It is sad and solemn that God the Father lashed the Messiah in our place. But how marvelous it is that through Jesus being bruised with stripes, we are healed of our sin sickness!

In *Messiah*, Handel masterfully has the singers repeat the words "And with his stripes we are healed" thirty-five times. This is serious repetition. He intertwines the singing of these words among the different sections of the choir. The entire chorus, which is made up of sopranos, altos, tenors, and basses, sings these words quickly, with the different vocal parts overlapping one another.

The repetition reminds us of how the lash fell repeatedly on the back of the Lord. The whip fell more than thirty-five times. Those painful stripes were instrumental in stripping away our sin and giving us healing.

The gospel writers tell us about the scourging of Jesus (Mark 15:15; John 19:1). The stripes laid upon Jesus came from cords or ropes with bits of metal or bone embedded in the ends. Jesus was flogged with these whips. The wounds they left were fiery, red, sensitive, and stinging. The bits of metal or bone tore open Jesus's flesh. It is possible that Jesus had flaps of loose skin hanging off His back. Such whipping was painful. The Romans did not have set limits on the number of lashes that could be meted out. Ancient prophecy predicted that the visage of the Messiah would be marred: "His visage was so marred more than any man, and his form more than the sons of men" (Isaiah 52:14). After Jesus was whipped, He was not recognizable. His face was swollen from the beating He took.

There is only one way to be healed of sin and its consequences. Only Jesus can heal our sin-sick souls, and only He can free us from shame and guilt. God had a sovereign purpose in laying these stripes on His Son. The Bible tells us that Jesus's suffering and crucifixion were planned by God. He was "delivered by the determinate counsel and foreknowledge of God" (Acts 2:23–24). God planned that Jesus would be flogged and that His people would receive healing.

How is it that the beating of Jesus can provide us with healing? Since God poured out His curse on the Messiah, I can receive God's blessings. The Messiah's suffering paid for my healing. In this life the Messiah can forgive my sins. In the world to come the Messiah will deliver me from any possible ill health. The leaves of the Tree of Life will be for the healing of the nations.

Christian, you are healed in principle. You will be fully healed when you receive your new, glorious body.

Thinking It Over

1. How can healing result from something so hurtful as "stripes"? How can we be healed by Christ's stripes?

2. What are the stripes to which the prophecy refers?

3. How does Christ heal us? What needs healing?

All We Like Sheep Have Gone Astray

*All we like sheep have gone astray; we have turned everyone to his own way;
and the LORD hath laid on him the iniquity of us all.*
—Isaiah 53:6

Handel has the choir sing the first words of this text as if they are sinful human beings who celebrate and delight in sin. They are happy to have wandered away from God. The high notes seem to convey a sense of elation at having found freedom apart from God. Our flesh believes that walking in our own way is the source of true bliss. But this false hope is stripped away by the sobering words: "And the Lord hath laid on him the iniquity of us all."

It is the deception of sin that leads straying sheep to celebrate their lostness. While eating poisonous plants, they imagine that they have never tasted a better feast. But there is also a clashing sound in the music that implies the tension between good and evil—and the tension of supposing that wandering brings true happiness.

There is a striking change of mood in the song when Handel introduces "and the Lord hath laid on him the iniquity of us all." I am surprised that Handel made such a contrast between the two parts of this text. If I were going to compose the music, I would have presented the lyrics about sheep having gone astray in a much more somber way.

Sheep need shepherds to lead them to pasture and to cool streams of water. They need a shepherd with a rod to defend them from wild animals and a staff to bring them back from their wandering.

By nature, God's people are straying sheep. They wander from the Good Shepherd and are easily lost. You and I, like sheep, have gone astray. We wander on dangerous paths. We do not follow the Good Shepherd but choose our own selfish way over God's. Although God's Word is to be our guide, we foolishly choose to do things our own foolish way. We chart our own path. We follow idolatrous dreams. The apostle Paul quotes a psalm that says "They are all gone out of the way" (Romans 3:1).

We still stray daily, choosing foolish ways that lead to destruction. Sin leads us far from God and into paths of bitterness, selfishness, pride, and greed. We wander away from God and feed on wicked entertainment. We eat the pleasures of sin. We enjoy imbibing books and movies that feed our pride and self-centeredness.

By nature we do not think that we need Jesus. We can protect ourselves. We can provide for ourselves. We don't think that we need to fear devilish wolves or Satan himself who goes about like a roaring lion.

Sheep have unique personalities. Some are timid while others are bold or curious. You and I have unique personalities too. Our sinful nature reveals itself through this personality. "We have turned every one to his own way." I stray in directions that you do not. Sin manifests itself in remarkably evil and tragic ways in our lives. It is awful how God's people, by nature, stray in so many crazy directions. We are inclined to follow the road that we think will make us happiest. Since you have different interests, goals, and passions than I, your own way will lead down a different path of sin.

I know that my Good Shepherd wants me to follow Him. He wants me to go where He directs. He wants me to love Him and remain close to Him. As I wash the floor, prepare food, and do the dishes and laundry, He wants me to follow Him. He wants my thoughts to be on Him and His graciousness, generosity, and faithfulness. He wants me to feed in the green pastures of His word. He does not want my mind to be filled with foolishness.

What a comfort it is that God has mercy on His wandering elect sheep! Scripture says that the Lord has laid all our sins on Christ.

The Lord laid all our sin on Jesus Christ! *"And the Lord hath laid on him the iniquity of us all."* The word *us* points to the atonement as particular redemption. The "us" for whom Christ atones are His elect people. The atonement is a limited atonement; God lays the iniquity of His elect (and only theirs) on Christ. The guilt of God's elect sheep was imputed to Christ. The Father had given these sheep to Jesus in the eternal decree of election. In the great exchange our guilt is imputed to Christ, and His innocence and righteousness are imputed to us through faith in Him. In 2 Corinthians 5:21 the Apostle Paul celebrates the Great Exchange: "For he hath made him to be sin for us, who knew no sin; that we might be made the righteousness of God in him."

Thinking It Over

1. How are you like a sheep?

2. How do you find yourself straying?

3. What negative consequences do you experience from your straying?

4. What kind of music does Handel use to accompany the lyrics in this text? What does his music communicate?

5. In what ways are you not tempted to stray?

6. What is the great exchange? (see 2 Corinthians 5:21)

All They That See Him, Laugh

All they that see me laugh me to scorn:
they shoot out the lip, they shake the head.
—Psalm 22:7

Psalm 22 is a prophecy about those who see and mock the Messiah. Laughing at someone is a form of ridicule. It is arrogant and condescending. We do not mock people we admire. We target people whom we do not like with ridicule.

The laughter of mockery

- works ill against your neighbor (Romans 13:10);
- doesn't display a compassionate heart (Colossians 3:12);
- doesn't show humility (Colossians 3:12);
- doesn't demonstrate brotherly affection (Romans 12:10);
- doesn't express harmony (Romans 12:16);
- doesn't show respect and honor (Romans 12:10).

Jesus was willing to suffer mockery. He came to be ridiculed. It was predicted that He would be mocked, and yet Messiah came.

During Jesus's ministry, He was mocked. When Jesus came to the home of the ruler of the synagogue whose daughter had died, He stated that the girl was not dead, but sleeping: "And they laughed him to scorn, knowing that she was dead. And he put them all out, and took her by the hand, and called, saying, Maid, arise. And her spirit came again, and she arose straightway: and he commanded to give her meat" (Luke 8:53–55).

At His Jewish trial, Jesus was blindfolded and slapped. The religious leaders mocked Jesus by asking who had hit Him. Luke records that the members of the Sanhedrin blasphemed Jesus.

During the Roman trial, soldiers derided Jesus. They stripped Jesus of His clothing and found a scarlet robe to place on Him. They thought that it was funny to dress Jesus up as a king. They laughed at placing a crown of thorns on His head. Laughing, they said, "Hail, king of the Jews!" They also thought it was funny to put a reed in Jesus's hands while they bowed before Him.

Later, as Jesus hung on the cross, the soldiers mocked Him saying, "If thou be the king of the Jews, save thyself" (Luke 23:37).

At the cross, people shot out their lips; they might have stuck out their tongues. Certainly they were conveying the same sort of mockery that children show when they stick out their tongues. Maybe they puckered their lips in implied criticism. People in the crowds wagged their heads. This communicates disapproval.

In the future every person will bow and every tongue will confess that Jesus is Messiah. Yet during His crucifixion, Jesus was mocked. The two thieves crucified with Him laughed at Him (Matthew 27:44). The religious rulers mocked Him. The crowds walking by laughed at Jesus.

Rich, smart, and powerful people laugh at us Christians. They ridicule us for not believing in evolutionary myths about origins. They laugh at the army of little white crosses that are set up to memorialize all of the babies aborted each year. They mock the moral scruples of Christians. They scorn us for not working on Sunday. They mock Christian music.

Unbelievers mock Christianity because the way of the kingdom of Christ is upside down and radically different from the world's way. Jesus's statements in Matthew 5 show the radical nature of His kingdom. Jesus calls the poor in spirit the blessed. He says that those who are reviled and slandered for His name are blessed.

The world laughed at Jesus. It laughs at us for the same reason.

Thinking It Over

1. For what Christian beliefs have you been mocked? Why?

2. For what Christian ethical views have you been mocked?

3. When was Jesus laughed at and mocked?

He Trusted in God

He trusted on the LORD that he would deliver him: let him deliver him, seeing he delighted in him.
—Psalm 22:8

At the cross, unbelieving Jews mocked the Messiah: "He trusted on the LORD that he would deliver him: let him deliver him, seeing he delighted in him."

Handel composed music for the chorus that sounds like people repeating these same mocking words: "He trusted on the Lord that he would deliver him." The bass sing these words to the tenors. The tenors sing to the altos. The altos share this message with the sopranos. And the sopranos sing these mocking words. Members of the Jewish crowds at Calvary laugh and shake their heads as they share these words with yet another person.

They cast scornful words at Jesus. They laugh at the possibility of God delivering Him. They are ignorant of the prophecies about the Messiah dying.

Jesus had claimed to have a unique relationship with God the Father. He got in trouble with the Jews for calling God His Father in a unique sense. So the crowds laughed about how Jesus claimed to trust His Father. And what has come of that!

But Jesus did trust His Father! Trust is dependence, a total confidence that you are safe. Jesus was fully confident in His Father's will. He perfectly trusted the Father to raise Him from the grave and to seat Him at His right hand. Since Jesus is one with the Father, He knew it was the Father's plan to bruise His Son for the salvation of His children. There was no other way to redeem a people for Himself.

I need to learn to trust God's plan for me, and you must learn to trust His plan for you. Do you find yourself, Christian friend, distrusting the Father's perfect plan? I find myself cast down about good plans I made that didn't turn out so well. I look at pictures of dear ones who are not walking with Christ and I tell myself, "Trust Him." I need to tell myself that God my Father is writing the story of the lives around me according to His sovereign will.

God's plan for our lives is perfect and His salvation is complete. Nothing needs to be added or subtracted. I must learn not to depend on myself for safety on earth or for entrance into heaven. I must know my utter need of Christ and have no confidence in the flesh.

I am untrustworthy and unable to keep myself healthy or safe. Whenever I am not trusting God, I am placing my trust in myself. I must tell myself, "Trust in the LORD with all thine heart; and lean not unto thine own understanding. In all thy ways acknowledge him, and he shall direct your paths. Be not wise in thine own eyes: fear the LORD, and depart from evil" (Proverbs 3:5–7). Trust is an act of faith. Throw yourself completely on Christ.

Jesus perfectly trusted the Father, and His perfect work is credited on my account. He did trust in God to deliver Him. I may fall very short of trusting Jesus, but His perfect trust becomes mine through faith in Him.

Thinking It Over

1. Why did the crowd at the cross share these mocking words about Jesus?

2. How did Jesus trust His Father?

3. What was the result of Jesus trusting His Father?

4. When is your faith challenged?

Thy Rebuke Hath Broken His Heart

Reproach hath broken my heart; and I am full of heaviness: and I looked for some to take pity, but there was none; and for comforters, but I found none.
—Psalm 69:20

Thy rebuke hath broken my heart; I am full of heaviness: I look for some to have pity on me, but there was no man, neither found I any to comfort me.
—Book of Common Prayer (1622), day 13, Psalm 69:21

The tenor solo for "Reproach has broken my heart" has the feel of a dirge (a sad and mournful song written in a minor key). The solo is unhurried and reflective. The Book of Common Prayer of 1622 states, "Thy rebuke hath broken my heart." The text from the Book of Common Prayer is different from the words in the King James Version, which reads, "Reproach hath broken my heart." My reflections on this text will take into consideration these two different readings.

The perfect Son of God suffered rebuke and reproach. He heard evil and untrue words spoken against Him. People walking by said, "Ah, thou that destroyest the temple, and buildest it in three days, save thyself and come down from the cross" (Mark 15:29–30). The chief priests mocked Him, saying, "He saved others; himself he cannot save" (Mark 15:31). He heard the thieves "cast the same in his teeth" (Matthew 27:44). These attacks caused mental agony for Christ, who was heartbroken by them. Ancient prophecy predicted that the Messiah would experience this: "Reproach hath broken my heart."

Jesus's heart is broken by reproach, and there was no one to help Him: "I looked for some to take pity, but there was none; and for comforters but I found none" (Psalm 69:20).

The women who served Him stood afar off. But where were His disciples when He wanted their encouragement? He desired someone to speak loving words of comfort, but no one pitied Him. The crowds who walked by the cross were pitiless.

Psalm 69:20 tells us that reproach has broken the Messiah's heart. The Book of Common Prayer switches this to "Thy rebuke hath broken my heart." The text of the psalm does not explicitly say that it is God's rebuke that breaks the Messiah's heart. The Book of Common Prayer reads into the text that it was the rebuke of God the Father that broke Jesus's heart. I think that it is the reproach of the crowds that the psalm has in mind.

But the wording of the Book of Common Prayer is theologically correct in that God the Father does pour out His wrath on the Messiah. Jesus appeased the wrath of God on the cross. That is why the apostle Paul calls the atonement "propitiation." It was a wrath-appeasing sacrifice. The apostle Peter writes about the Messiah, "Who his own self bare our sins in his own body on the tree" (1 Peter 2:24). Jesus was separated from fellowship with the Father and cried out, "Why hast thou forsaken me?" (Mark 15:34). We cannot understand the tremendous sorrow and agony Jesus experienced on the cross.

Lord's Day 15 in the Heidelberg Catechism asks what we mean in the Apostles' Creed when we say that Jesus "suffered under Pontius Pilate." The answer is,

> That during his whole life on earth, but especially at the end, Christ sustained in body and soul the wrath of God against the sin of the whole human race. This he did in order that, by his suffering as the only atoning sacrifice, he might deliver us, body and soul, from eternal condemnation, and gain for us God's grace, righteousness, and eternal life.

So even though the psalmist is probably referring to the reproaches of wicked men, it is true that the rebuke of the Father, as Christ was made sin for us, was a terrible sorrow.

Thinking It Over

1. What is the difference between the lyrics in *Messiah* and the text in Psalm 69:20?

2. What does it mean that reproach *broke Christ's heart*?

3. Who showed pity to Jesus while He hung on His cross?

4. Did God rebuke Jesus? What might that have involved?

Behold and See

Behold, and see if there be any sorrow like unto my sorrow.
—Lamentations 1:12

Lamentations is a book of weeping and lament. The prophet Jeremiah wept for the city of Jerusalem. The beautiful city of God was burned. The citizens had been taken captive by the Babylonians. Jeremiah closely identified himself with the city of Jerusalem. It is hard to distinguish between Jeremiah's tears and the sorrow of the city.

Jeremiah preached to covenant people who would not listen to his message. He was beaten and put in stocks. A king burned a scroll containing his prophecies. A king threw him into a dungeon, where he sank down into the mire. The leadership in Judah claimed that he deserved death for supporting the enemy because he prophesied that Judah would be defeated.

The Bible tells us God sympathized with His people's suffering. He felt their pain and used His everlasting arms to protect and carry them. "In all their affliction he was afflicted" (Isaiah 63:9).

Jeremiah grieved over how the holy city that once was filled with hundreds of pilgrims on festive days now lay empty. The beautiful city of God had lost her former glory. Her sanctuary was defiled by the heathens.

When Jesus thought about what would happen to Jerusalem, He also wept: "And when he was come near, he beheld the city, and wept over it" (Luke 19:41). Jesus knew what calamities the Romans would visit on Jerusalem.

The words of Jeremiah in Lamentations become the words of the Messiah: "Behold, and see if there be any sorrow like unto my sorrow." The weeping of Jeremiah is a picture of the sorrow of Christ. The music is written in a minor key, which best portrays sadness and sorrow.

Jesus's sorrow was not limited to His grief about the calamity that would be visited on Jerusalem. He was a man of sorrows. He suffered the sorrows of being "made sin" for His people. Look at the distress of Jesus in the garden of Gethsemane (Luke 22:39-48).

We should be grateful that Christ came into this world as a man of sorrows. Christ suffered great sorrows so that we might have great joy. As we sing in "When I Survey the Wondrous Cross," what Christ has done "demands my soul, my life, my all." Love Christ. Do what He commands. Go where He sends you. Act as He demands. Forgive as the Messiah has forgiven you. Show pity as the Messiah has pitied you.

Thinking It Over

1. Why did Jeremiah have such great sorrow?

2. Why is Jesus called a "man of sorrows"

He Was Cut Off Out of the Land

He was cut off out of the land of the living: for the transgression of my people was he stricken.
—Isaiah 53:8

Isaiah predicts that the Messiah would be "cut off out of the land of the living." The Bible uses the phrase "cut off" over 190 times. Our Savior needed to be "cut off" in order that we would never be cut off.

Handel communicates the idea of being "cut off" in his music. He places a sixteenth rest following the singing of the words "cut off." The abrupt break communicates the effect of something being severed.

The Messiah was cut off out of the land of the living. It is shocking that the Messiah is cut off. One might have thought that the covenant people would have welcomed the arrival of the messianic prince.

God dwelt with His people in Jerusalem. The temple was the house of God. The prophetess Anna spent her days in the temple because it symbolized fellowship and communion with God. Because the temple was located there, Jerusalem was the city of God.

This helps us to understand the gravity of Jesus being expelled from the Holy City. When Jesus was led outside of the city of Jerusalem to be crucified, He was being expelled from the city of God. Jesus was cut off from the land of the living by being expelled from Jerusalem and crucified.

Crucifixion was a form of punishment in which the victim was no longer on earth, but neither was he in heaven. He hung between the two. Crucifixion symbolized that the crucified one was rejected by heaven and earth, cut off from heaven and earth.

Why did this "cutting off" need to happen? Jesus was cut off from the land of the living so that we might be able to enjoy the presence of God.

We deserve to be cut off from the land of the living for our sins. The wages of sin is death. Jesus was cut off in order to pay for the following sins that we have committed and which were imputed to Christ in the great exchange:

- twisting the truth
- ignoring others
- lacking in hospitality
- selfishness
- harshness
- gossip
- lying
- covetousness
- gluttony
- wasting time
- deceit
- cutting down people
- cursing
- taking God's name in vain
- evil thoughts
- sexual impurity
- a dirty mouth
- taking advantage of others
- dishonesty
- hatred
- stealing
- unthankfulness
- fear

- discontentment
- dishonoring those in authority
- unmerciful
- drunkenness
- cheating
- whispering about others
- impatience
- anxiety
- immodesty
- greed
- being angry
- being unforgiving
- not trusting God
- despising God's word
- not loving my neighbor as myself
- idolatry
- having selfish ambition
- lust
- being ashamed of Jesus
- bitterness
- complaining
- speaking evil of others
- giving grudgingly
- denying Jesus as the Messiah
- disobedient
- not doing what God commands
- being lazy
- murmuring
- not keeping the Lord's Day holy
- not loving God with all my heart soul and mind

Thinking It Over

1. Circle the above sins that you need to confess to God.

2. Find a verse from the Bible that you could memorize or write on a card to help you flee that sin.

3. What does it mean to be "cut off from the land of the living"

4. How was Jesus cut off?

But Thou Didst Not Leave

For thou wilt not leave my soul in hell;
neither wilt thou suffer thine Holy One to see corruption.
—Psalm 16:10

Handel took the liberty of adding the word *but* to the text of Psalm 16:10 instead of beginning with the word *for*, as in the King James Version. He wanted to create a contrast between this song and the prior tenor recitative. Jesus, the one who was rebuked and who looked for pity, was not left forgotten by God.

God would not leave the Messiah's soul in hell. There is one who will show pity to the Messiah, although He will not show this pity until the Messiah can cry, "It is finished!" Once the Messiah had satisfied the justice of God, the Father showed His delight in His beloved Son. The Father would not leave the soul of the Messiah in hell.

As a true man, Jesus possessed both a human body and a human soul. He needed to have a human soul in order to be a true and complete man. Our soul (or spirit) is the center of spiritual life. Our soul is the part of us that can survive our death. At the moment of death, our soul is carried by the angels to paradise.

On the cross, Jesus commended His human "spirit" to the Father: "Father, into thy hands I commend my spirit: and having said thus, he gave up the ghost" (Luke 23: 46). Jesus's body went into the grave, and His spirit/soul went to the Father.

God the Father would not allow Jesus's body to stay in "hell." Because of the perfect obedience of His beloved Son, God the Father would raise the Messiah victoriously from the grave.

The word *hell* is a translation of the Hebrew word *sheol*, which refers to the grave or the place of the dead. So *hell* refers to the tomb where Jesus's body was buried. *Hell* here does not refer to the lake of fire. It was while Jesus hung on the cross that He suffered hellish agonies—although He never physically visited the place that is hell.

God would raise the Messiah from the tomb on Sunday morning.

The grave is the place of corruption. God the Father would not allow Jesus's body to decay and rot in the earth. The process of decomposition was interrupted by the resurrection. Jesus's body did not return to the dust.

It is striking that the prophecy identified the Messiah as the "holy one." It is true that the Messiah was made sin for His people. In His state of humiliation, God had imputed the guilt of God's people to the Messiah. But Christ was able to save us because He was personally holy. He never committed a single sin.

Because of the holiness and perfect obedience of the Messiah, God the Father will not allow His body to turn back to the dust. God raised the Messiah on Easter morning. He gave to the Christ a new, glorious resurrection body.

Thinking It Over

1. What or where is the "hell" in which the Messiah's soul would not be left?

2. What would God not allow to happen to the Messiah? What is the "corruption" mentioned?

3. Why is the Messiah called the "holy one"?

Lift Up Your Heads, O Ye Gates

*Lift up your heads, O ye gates; and be lift up, ye everlasting doors;
and the King of glory shall come in. Who is this King of glory? The LORD strong
and mighty, the LORD mighty in battle. Lift up your heads, O ye gates; even
lift them up, ye everlasting doors; and the King of glory shall come in. Who is
this King of glory? The LORD of hosts, he is the King of glory.*
—Psalm 24:7–10

Listen to a poem that I wrote based on Psalm 24:7-10:

Look up!
Swing wide the doors!
See the glorious One!
The King of Glory,
He Shall come in!
Yes!
He Shall come in!

David and the Israelites
brought the ark
up to the mountain
with gladness and shouting
with instruments and offerings
David offered them a psalm
O thanks to God.

&

Look up!
Swing wide the doors!
See the glorious One!
The King of Glory,
He Shall come in!

Yes!
He Shall come in!

Jesus rode Jerusalem's streeta
Arrayed on a colt.
The crowds threw down
Their coats and palms
and shouted
hosannas to the King
who comes in God's name!

₰

Look up!
Swing wide the doors!
Set the glorious one!
The King of Glory,
He shall come in!
Yes!
He shall come in!

The gates and doors of heaven
stand erect to meet the King
They rise. Allowing entrance
to Jesus Christ,
the King of Glory
ascended
and exalted.

&

Look up!
See the glorious One!
The rightful King,
The Lord of Hosts!
He has entered Heaven
and reigns
at the right hand of God!

Thinking It Over

1. How can gates lift up their heads?

2. Why is Jesus called the King of "glory"?

3. What event is being described in this prophecy (See Psalm 68:18, Luke 24:51-52, Acts 1:9, Eph 4:8 and 1 Peter 3:22) ?

Unto Which of the Angels Said He

For unto which of the angels said he at any time, Thou art my Son,
this day have I begotten thee?
—Hebrews 1:5

These lyrics are often left out in performances of *Messiah*. I listened to a number of performances of *Messiah* on CDs and online and discovered that this text is not sung in any of them. Conductors need to make decisions about omitting portions of the oratorio in the interest of time. Many performances of *Messiah* include an intermission because otherwise the performance can go on for too long.

In this oft-omitted portion, the tenor recites a rhetorical question from the book of Hebrews. Since this verse gives a beautiful defense of who Jesus Christ is, it should not be overlooked. Jesus's divinity was attacked in the early church by the Arian heretics. Today, cults like the Jehovah's Witnesses and Mormons deny that Jesus is truly God. The Unitarian Universalists claim that the Son is a created being.

An important theologian of the fourth century, Athanasius argued a long time ago that the Messiah can save only if He is God. It was prophesied that the Messiah would be God incarnate.

The author of Hebrews celebrates the exalted deity of Christ and His superiority to the angels. In comparing the angels, which are creatures, to the Messiah, the writer to the Hebrews states: "For unto which of the angels said he at any time, Thou art my Son, this day have I begotten thee?" The answer to this rhetorical question is that God never spoke these high words to any angel. This is a quote of David from Psalm 2:7.

Angels are celestial beings created as messengers of God and servants to those who are heirs of the kingdom. They do not mediate between us and God. They are creatures who are far inferior to the Son of God, the great messenger of the covenant. The angels worship the Son of God. Christ sends them on missions to protect His elect and to carry out His purposes. At the close of history, God will commission angels to gather the elect.

The Messiah is preeminent above the angels. At Jesus's baptism, God the Father said, "Thou art my beloved Son; in thee I am well pleased" (Luke 3:22). There is no place in Scripture where angels are spoken of in this way.

In his first chapter, the writer to the Hebrews tells us why Jesus is supreme—far greater than any angels:

- Jesus has been "appointed heir of all things" (v. 2).
- Jesus is the one "by whom also he made the worlds" (v. 2).
- Jesus is "the brightness of his glory" (v. 3).
- Jesus is "the express image of his person" (v. 3).
- Jesus is "upholding all things by the word of his power"(v.3).
- Jesus has "a more excellent name," begotten Son (vv. 4–5).
- Jesus is the object of the angels' worship (v. 6).
- Jesus reigns on the throne forever (v. 8).
- Jesus is Creator (v. 10).
- Jesus is seated at God's right hand (v. 13).
- Jesus sends forth angels to be His messengers (v. 14).

Jesus is the eternal begotten Son of God. We confess this when we recite the Apostles' Creed. We say, "I believe in Jesus Christ, His only begotten Son, our Lord." Jesus is the second person of the holy Trinity.

If Jesus is and always has been the eternal and natural Son of God, why does the text say, "This day I have begotten thee"? These words can be spoken about the Son by God the Father because the triune God lives outside of time. Jesus is and always remains the Son of God. There is no beginning or end to His sonship. He is the same yesterday, today, and forever (Hebrews 13:8)!

The Son of God is eternally begotten, not made. The text does not say that God the Father created the Son. Rather, it speaks about the Father begetting His Son. That is why the Nicene Creed emphasizes that the Son was begotten, not made. The Father eternally generated His Son. Just like an earthly father begets a son in his image and likeness with a wife, God the Father (without a wife) generates His beloved Son. While an earthly son is an imperfect picture of his dad, the Son is the perfect image of His Father.

Thinking It Over

1. How is the Messiah greater than the angels?

2. What does it mean that the Father has "begotten" His Son?

3. How can the Father speak about a "day" in which He begot the Son?

4. What is Arianism?

5. If confronted by a member of a cult who believed in Arianism, how would you defend the deity of the Messiah?

Let All the Angels of God Worship Him

And let all the angels of God worship him.
—Hebrews 1:6

Although this chorus "Let All the Angels of God Worship Him" is generally omitted from many performances of *Messiah*, I cannot omit some reflections on it. What exhilarating words these are! They are especially exhilarating in the context of the entire oratorio. The oratorio moves the Christian to praise. And we certainly want the angels of God to worship the Messiah. They did at His birth on the outskirts of Bethlehem. As we begin to perceive the glory of the Messiah, we want Him to be celebrated by the holy angels.

The word *angel* literally means "messenger." God calls the angels "messengers" because in sacred history God sent messages to His people through them.

At significant times in the history of His church, God sent angels. He commissioned them to announce the births of significant men in the history of salvation. They appeared at unique times in sacred history to communicate prophecy, as, for example, in the case of Gabriel's visit to Daniel. We find angels appearing at momentous moments in history. Here are some examples of angelic appearances for significant events in sacred history:

- Angels sang at the creation of the world.
- Angels appeared to Abraham several times; they are best known for stopping him from sacrificing his son Isaac.
- An angel met Jacob on his way to Padan-aram.
- Angels made several appearances to the judges.

- Angels visited Zacharias, Joseph, and Mary.
- Angels appeared and sang at the birth of Jesus.
- Angels were present at the tomb after Jesus arose.
- An angel appeared to Peter in prison.
- An angel met Philip and led him to preach and baptize an Ethiopian.
- An angel appeared to Cornelius, a Gentile.
- Angels will gather the elect at the end of history.

Angels are called to important work. Michael, an archangel, protects the covenant people. Angels serve God's people and protect covenant children. But the greatest calling that angels have is to worship God.

God created the angels to adore Him. That is why you will always find angels before the throne of God. Angels fall on their faces before the One seated on the throne. The triune God is always the object of their worship. The apostle John gets a glimpse of this: "All the angels stood round about the throne, and about the elders and the four beasts, and fell before the throne on their faces, and worshipped God, saying, Amen: Blessing, and glory, and wisdom, and thanksgiving, and honour, and power, and might, be unto our God forever and ever. Amen" (Revelation 7:11–12).

The Greek word for *worship* literally means "to bow down." Worship is bowing down in physical submission before the King of kings. The angels are called on to adore, love, honor, and praise the eternal King.

The Christian joins in the desire that all the angels would praise the Messiah. "Let all" communicates the desire that each one of the millions of angels might bow before their Creator. In a vision Daniel sees ten thousand times ten thousand angels serving God. Imagine seeing one hundred million angels serving and worshiping the King of the universe! Thousands upon thousands of angels cry out, "Worthy is the Lamb that was slain to receive power, and riches, and wisdom, and strength, and honour, and glory, and blessing" (Revelation 5:12).

And we will not keep silent. We want to join with the angels. We do not want to exhort all the angels to worship the Lord while we remain silent ourselves. We say, along with David, "I will extol thee, my God, O king; and I will bless thy name for ever and ever. Every day will I bless thee; and I will praise thy name for ever and ever" (Psalm 145:1).

Thinking It Over

1. At what significant points in sacred history have angels appeared to men?

2. What does the word *angel* literally mean?

3. What does it mean to "worship" God?

4. Where are visits of the angel Gabriel recorded in the Bible (in what Bible stories)?

5. How do the different kinds of angels (seraphim, cherubim, and angels) worship and serve God (See Psalm 91:11, Acts 27:23, Hebrews 1:4, Genesis 3:24, Ezekiel 10, Isaiah 6:2, 6 and consult a Bible dictionary)?

Thou Art Gone Up on High

Thou hast ascended on high, thou hast led captivity captive: thou hast received gifts for men; yea, for the rebellious also, that the LORD God might dwell among them.
—Psalm 68:18

Maybe you know some of the lyrics and tunes of *Messiah* by heart. I walk around the house singing some of the pieces. But when I came to the text that is Psalm 68:18, I couldn't recall how the music went. I suppose it is because this piece is often omitted in performances of *Messiah*.

Forty days after Jesus arose, an amazing event happened at the Mount of Olivet. It forever changed the course of history. Jesus departed from His disciples and ascended into heaven.

At this moment, the Messiah is sitting at God's right hand, governing everything on land or in the sea. Jesus ascended on high and was set at God's right hand in heavenly places. Paul writes that the Messiah is now "far above all principality, and power, and might, and dominion, and every name that is named, not only in this world, but also in that which is to come: and hath put all things under his feet, and gave him to be the head over all things to the church, which is his body the fullness of him that filleth all in all" (Ephesians 1:21–22).

God has put all things under the Messiah's feet. He governs everything. He is supreme over the cold, the snow, and the rain. He commands the storm. He sends the hurricane off the coast. The earth quakes at His command. The wind and the sea obey Him.

Jesus, our advocate, mediates with the Father on our behalf. The Messiah will not allow any human being or devil to bring a charge against His elect.

In heaven, the Messiah is praying for His people. He intercedes with the Father on our behalf. He prays for grace and forgiveness for us. He prays that our faith would be strengthened. And the Father always hears His intercessory prayers.

Since the Messiah knows God's eternal plan, Jesus entreats our Father for good gifts to be given to us in accordance with His plan. He asks for grace for every situation and circumstance that comes our way. God's Son knows that we need protection, so He intercedes for us. And we remain clueless about these prayers and how they are constantly being answered. We receive many benefits without being aware that the Messiah asked for them.

From heaven, the ascended Messiah sends His Spirit. He causes His Spirit to indwell His people. The reason why we can walk in gentleness and be patient is because the Holy Spirit has been poured out in our lives.

Another benefit that we receive from Jesus's ascension is that we are defended and preserved from our enemies. The Devil desires to catch us in snares, but Jesus puts a hedge of protection around us. Why is it that temptations lose their power? Christ's mighty Spirit protects us from mighty temptations.

Jesus's ascension is like a deposit you put down on a car or a house. The deposit holds the item for you. Christ's bodily presence in heaven is the guarantee His people will also enjoy paradise in the future.

Jesus takes captive those who formerly had been taken captive by sin. Jesus made the point that we fallen humans do not just sin, but we are slaves to sin. The Messiah buys us back. He frees rebellious, hateful, lawbreakers from bondage to sin and the Devil. This captivity of the captives is a release from the bondage of sin and involves true freedom, the freedom of being the adoptive children of God.

For thirty-three years Jesus lived among the captives, and now He indwells them by His Holy Spirit. He is truly Immanuel, God with us!

He purchased for us gifts by His death—the gifts of grace, mercy, love, salvation, forgiveness, peace, and joy. The end result is that God dwells among us. The God of the universe now indwells His people. This wonder is the result of the ascension of the Messiah and the fact that He has poured out His Spirit.

Thinking It Over

1. What does it mean that the Messiah has "ascended on high"?

2. How does the ascension of Jesus benefit us?

3. What does it mean that Jesus leads captivity captive?

4. How is Jesus's ascension like a deposit?

The Lord Gave the Word

The Lord gave the word: great was the company of those that published it.
—Psalm 68:11

You might be familiar with these lyrics of *Messiah*: "The Lord gave the word: great was the company of the preachers" (see Psalm 68:11). I was surprised when I looked in my King James Bible and found the translation of Psalm 68:11 shown above. There is a difference between the King James Version and the English Book of Common Prayer from which Handel partially acquired his lyrics. The difference lies in the reference to the company of the "preachers" rather than to the company of "those that published it."

I discovered that the Hebrew text does not have either the idea of preachers or an abstract reference to "those that published it." The Hebrew text reads, "The Lord gave the word: great was the *host of women* who published it. The psalmist is singing about women who publish the good news of God's Word.

So Psalm 68:11 does not refer to men preachers. It refers to ladies, daughters of Zion, who are publishing some message from God.

Even though Psalm 68:11 does not refer to preachers, it certainly is true, as the Book of Common Prayer implies, that the company of preachers is great. There is a great company of those who are preaching the word. There are so many people who need to hear the word of God that there must be a great number of preachers. Every generation needs young men to join the company of preachers. Your generation needs the gospel just like the previous generations. If you are a qualified young man, prayerfully consider whether God is calling you to gospel ministry.

But since the text behind the lyrics in *Messiah* refers to women who publish a message, we need to talk about what this means and involves. The context is one in which Jewish women celebrate a divine victory. The idea continues in Psalm 68:12 where the Hebrew literally speaks of beautiful women who divide the spoil.

The Israelite women happily shared the victory of their army. A messenger would arrive with news of the latest Israelite victory. Women would delight in passing on the good report to their neighbors. Men returned to their homes tired out from the battle. Women would divide the spoil among the covenant families. When the women talked about the victory of Israel, they really celebrated the conquest of God.

God fought for His people at the Red Sea, drowning Pharaoh and his hosts. On hearing of the victory of the men in battle, the Israelite women would run from tent to tent celebrating the good news. The women took timbrels and danced. Do you remember Miriam's song? "Sing ye to the LORD, for he hath triumphed gloriously; the horse and his rider hath he thrown into the sea" (Exodus 15:21).

After a battle with the Philistines, women came out singing and dancing with their tambourines. They celebrated the triumph: "And the women answered one another as they played, and said, Saul has slain his thousands, and David his ten thousands" (1 Samuel 18:7).

God gave "the word" to be published. It is not to be kept secret! Portions of the Bible have been translated in over thirty-three hundred languages. North Korea has banned the Bible, but Christians release balloons that carry portions of Scripture across the border into the country. In the last three centuries the Lord has opened doors for world missions. Yet millions of people remain unreached by the gospel.

Are you celebrating the victory of Christ?
Have you internalized the depths of this magnificent victory?
Do you realize from what you have been saved?
Then by all means praise the One who has defeated the enemy! Our souls should find such delight that we break into song. Your name should be listed among the great company of those who publish the word. A stanza from a song that is a paraphrase of Psalm 47 exhorts the believer,

> Take a psalm and shout,
> Let His praise ring out;
> Lift your voice and sing
> Glory to our King;
> He is Lord of earth,
> Magnify His worth.

God continued using women like Mary Magdalene; Joanna; and Mary, the mother of James, to share the news of the resurrected and triumphant Christ. The women returned from the sepulcher to publish the good news that their Master was risen.

This setting of Psalm 89 expresses the greatness of the Lord:

> How blessed, Lord, are they who know the joyful sound,
> Who, when they hear Thy voice, in happiness abound!
> With steadfast step they walk, their countenances beaming
> With brightness of the light that from Thy face is streaming;
> Exalted by Thy might from depths of desolation,
> They praise fore'er Thy Name, Thy justice and salvation.

Thinking It Over

1. According to the Hebrew text, who published the word?

2. Why is it fitting to apply this text to ordained preachers?

3. How can you publish the word?

How Beautiful Are the Feet of Them

How beautiful are the feet of them that preach the gospel of peace, and bring glad tidings of good things!
—Romans 10:15

Have you ever considered how important your feet are? We use our feet all day long, and yet they are one of the least-cared-for members of our body. Our feet take us places and help us get around. We need our feet to get out of bed in the morning.

The feet of pastors who preach the gospel of peace are beautiful. Why? It is not an outward beauty. In fact, most pastors would not want you to see their feet. The beauty has to do with the task of their feet. The foot of a preacher is beautiful because he takes up the task of mounting the steps to the pulpit every Sunday. My husband's feet are beautiful. Why? It is his foot that operates the car that brings him to the prison to minister to and instruct prisoners in the good news of the gospel. My uncle's feet are beautiful. Why? Those feet boarded an airplane to Singapore to preach Christ. The feet of preachers that bring glad tidings of good things are beautiful.

In Romans 10, Paul is describing the way in which people come to faith in Christ. It is through the preaching of the word that men, women, and children are saved. The company of preachers is those sent by God to bring the good news of the gospel. The office of minister, or preacher, is not the office of every believer, but God commissions men to this special office. All believers assist the preacher as they witness about what Jesus Christ has done for them.

Thinking It Over

1. Why are the feet of preachers called beautiful?

2. How are your feet beautiful?

Their Sound Is Gone Out

Their sound went into all the earth, and their words unto the ends of the world.
—Romans 10:18

An old yellow, tattered map fell from a book I was paging through. I carefully unfolded it and noticed it wasn't just any old map. It was a printed copy of the central portion of Africa, the way David Livingstone surveyed it in 1866 to 1873. A red line traced his journeys back and forth across large portions of the continent.

How is it that hard-to-find places on the globe have vibrant Christians? How is it that Amerindians have come to faith in Christ? Why are there missionaries in China? The words of gospel preachers have gone to the ends of the world.

As a young Scottish man, David Livingstone (1813–1873) set his sights on being a medical missionary to the dark and mysterious continent of Africa. On board the ship to Africa, he learned about navigation. He landed near present-day Port Elizabeth in South Africa. He crossed mountains and blazed across Africa. He wanted to find a river that could provide a waterway for transport from inland Africa to the coast so that he could help Africans engage in commerce. He hoped that then they wouldn't rely on slavery, which he wanted to end. He believed that encouraging trade would provide alternate means for Africans to develop economies that were not dependent on slaves. Livingstone was outraged by the idea of a person selling a fellow human being.

What brought this man to the far-off continent of Africa? Why would he learn fourteen African languages? Why would he trudge through the dry and thirsty Kalahari Desert? Why did he endure "the fever" (malaria)? Why would he willingly live in a tent for thirty years? Why would he endure things like a lion attack?

Livingstone lived to tell Sebituane, an African chief, about Jesus Christ. He requested a mission station to be set up in the area where Sebituane ruled. His travels and discoveries opened the way for other missionaries to follow. He opened routes into unknown south central Africa. For many years Livingstone explored rather than preached. His explorations benefited future missionaries.

Why would David Brainerd (1718–1747) spend his short life of twenty-nine years bringing the gospel to the Delaware Indians of New Jersey? God gave him a heart willing to bring the gospel to a fierce tribe. He was willing to preach and teach, although he had frequent coughing spells, coughing up blood because of tuberculosis. His desire that the Indians would come to faith in Jesus Christ was so strong that although he was often despondent because of depression, he pressed on. Brainerd traveled thousands of miles on horseback. He ate a lot of boiled corn and hasty pudding. He lived a lonely life because of his desire to bring the gospel to the Amerindians.

The Bible says: "Their sound went into all the earth, and their words unto the ends of the world." Since the sound of God's preachers needs to go to the ends of the earth, American missionary Adoniram Judson (1788–1850) learned the difficult Burmese language, with its circular letters. He suffered brutal imprisonment. He lost a baby and then his first wife. And this was only the beginning of his sufferings.

William Carey (1761-1834) was a British missionary to Calcutta, India. Contemplate the great message he desired to bring to India! He would keep his eye on Christ through the huge loss he felt when his wife dies and a fire destroyed 15 years of Bible translation work.

Hudson Taylor (1832–1905), an Englishman, willingly moved to China. He dressed like a native in a long congee and even wore his hair in a long, demeaning pigtail.

These missionaries engaged in world missions because they knew that God uses the means of the gospel preached to save sinners.

Every Christmas my parents would send a package that included a rum-soaked fruitcake to the missionaries in Jamaica whom our church supported. This little act of kindness communicated, "You have beautiful feet. Thank you for sharing the gospel of peace."

Thinking It Over

1. Use the internet to research the life of Hudson Taylor. What trials and hardships did he endure for the sake of Christ? Include details about his travels, wives, children, and converts.

2. Use the internet to research the life of Adoniram Judson. What trials and hardships did he endure for the sake of Christ? Include details about his travels, wives, children, and converts.

3. Use the internet to research the life of William Carey. What trials and hardships did he endure for the sake of Christ? Include details about his travels, wives, children, and converts.

4. What missionaries do you support? How can you encourage this missionary?

Why Do the Nations Rage

Why do the heathen rage, and the people imagine a vain thing?
The kings of the earth set themselves, and the rulers take counsel together,
against the LORD, and against his anointed, saying. . .
—Psalm 2:1–2

Have you ever watched a parent try to place an undisciplined child in a grocery cart? The little tyke's body twists and turns, writhing in the most curious positions. Why all this screaming and fussing? Toddlers want to be in control.

World rulers also rage and fuss. They believe that they should be above accountability. They do not want to be subject to God or to His laws. They make plans, expecting things to go their way. They plot and take counsel to ensure that they win. These ungodly rulers are full of conceit and arrogance. They imagine that they are in sovereign control of the land that they rule. They do as they please. They fight against the Lord's anointed.

Leaders have made rules against God and His perfect laws. Look at the contrast between what God demands and what wicked men support:

God's law says, "Thou shalt not kill."	They allow abortion.
God says, "Honor your father and mother."	They legalize euthanasia.

God says, "Keep the Sabbath day holy."	They say, "Let them work!"
God says marriage is between one man and one woman.	They say, "Marriage is also two men or two women."

In Acts 3:6, a forty-year-old man who had been lame from birth was commanded, "In the name of Jesus Christ of Nazareth, rise up and walk." In Acts 4, the leaders arrested Peter and John for playing a role in healing this man. Later, the rulers released the apostles.

When Peter and John gathered with the early Christians, they addressed God in prayer as "Lord, thou art God, which hast made heaven, and the earth, and the sea, and all that in them is" (Acts 4:24). Peter and John praised God's sovereign rule and even quoted Psalm 2:1–2. They rehearsed how Herod and Pontius Pilate had raged against Jesus: "For of a truth against thy holy child Jesus, whom thou hast anointed, both Herod and Pontius Pilate, with the Gentiles, and the people of Israel, were gathered together" (Acts 4:27).

God was supreme over the two great rulers who put Jesus to death. God ordained that these rulers would reject His Son.

Things haven't changed today. Kim Jong Un is a present-day example of a ruler who rages against the Lord. This current leader of North Korea demands that he and his ancestors be treated as gods. He insists that his photo be in every home. He brainwashes children to worship him and his regime. He is an antichrist. He rages against God. He imprisons and murders Christians. He will not allow Bibles in the country. He doesn't kiss the Son of God, as the psalmist warns rulers to do in Psalm 2:12.

Why do The Nations Rage

Thinking It Over

1. Use the passages below to explain how Herod and Pontius Pilate raged against the Lord.

Herod Luke 23:11	
Pontius Pilate John 19:13–22	

2. List rulers in the Bible who ranted and raved against the Lord.

3. What happened to these rulers in Bible times who raved against the Lord?

4. List another world ruler who is currently taking counsel against the Lord and explain his or her tactics.

Let Us Break Their Bonds Asunder

Let us break their bands asunder, and cast away their cords from us.
—Psalm 2:3

Handel created four pieces of music for the lyrics that come from Psalm 2. Each one of the four lyrics has a common theme: the wicked kings of the earth try to free themselves from the lordship of the Messiah. The structure of both the music and words in the chorus, "Let us break their bands asunder, and cast away their cords from us," are memorable. The music communicates the idea that the nations are trying to rip away the cords that bind them. Handel portrays the kings and nations as trying repeatedly to break their bands asunder. But they have no success.

In the Bible we find wicked men speaking in the first person plural, saying, "Let us." We find this brief phrase already in Genesis 11 when fallen man rebels against God by trying to build the Tower of Babel. Three times fallen men are recorded as saying, "Let us":

1. "And they said to one another, Go to, *let us* make brick, and burn them thoroughly" (Genesis 11:3).
2.
3. "And they said, Go to *let us* build a city and a tower, whose top may reach unto heaven" (Genesis 11:4).

4. "And *let us* make us a name, lest we be scattered abroad upon the face of the whole earth" (Genesis 11:4, emphases added).

Their threefold desire is to make bricks, a city, and a name. Their plans are out of sync with God's desire that mankind would multiply and fill the earth (Genesis 9:1). These three uses of "let us" give us insight into fallen man's desires. The wicked nations are like an unruly fugitive who tries to break out of the handcuffs that bind his wrists. They desire freedom from God's law. They are not happy that in the way of breaking God's commandments there is judgment.

It is interesting that in response to fallen mankind at the Tower of Babel trying to build a tower to heaven, God Himself uses similar language: "And the LORD said . . . Go to, *let us* go down, and there confound their language, that they may not understand one another's speech" (Genesis 11:6–7).

By nature we do not like the law of love. We do not want to be constrained to do everything for the glory of God. We do not want to love our neighbor who is mean to us. The wicked want to break any moral bands that constrict their freedom to sin.

Thinking It Over

1. Do you ever have the desire to get out from under God's law? What laws do you wish were not in effect?

2. Give an example of a law of God and how God gave us the law for our good and happiness.

3. In the twenty-first century, what laws of God are especially repugnant to the wicked?

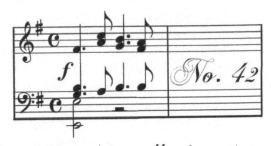

He That Dwelleth in Heaven

He that sitteth in the heavens shall laugh: the Lord shall have
them in derision.
—Psalm 2:4

In a recitative, the tenor soloist states, "He that sitteth in the heavens shall laugh: the Lord shall have them in derision." The text is short and pithy but speaks volumes. The range of notes the tenor sings conveys the exalted throne of the One who sits laughing in heaven. As the notes plunge downward, Handel communicates God's scorn and derision.

Our sovereign Lord laughs at those who take counsel against Him. This laughter is not the laughter of lighthearted, jovial amusement. It is the mocking laughter of the righteous King.

God calmly sits and laughs at the wicked. He is not distraught at the rebellion of sinful rulers. He can laugh because every ounce of power that human rulers possess is given to them by God. He gives authority to rulers and takes it away. God mocks kings who try to break away from His law. Imagine a little black ant thinking in its insect brain that it can win an arm-wrestling match against a human. The idea that the rulers of the earth would try to challenge God's throne brings mocking laughter to the mouth of God. God can speak one little word, and an earthly ruler is deposed. God has already decreed the day of death of the wicked ruler. He is preparing the ruler for judgment.

God laughs because He knows that foolish rulers know He is and yet live in self-denial. They know from general revelation that God is. They sense God's power and Godhead every time they walk under the starry sky. Yet they repress this knowledge and imagine that they can reject God's authority and survive.

The kings of the earth know from their conscience that there is right and wrong. As dictators publish new laws, they know that there is a divine lawgiver. While earthly kings are unjust, the King of heaven is perfectly righteous. And He will hold the kings of earth responsible.

As the one true God who is supreme in the world He created and who will execute perfect justice in His judgment of the kings of the earth, "the Lord shall hold them in derision." God holds the wicked in disdain and contempt. He speaks to them in His wrath. And God's curse is effectual. God's words of judgment will be carried out. And the wicked will pay.

Thinking It Over

1. Does God laugh? What causes God to laugh at wicked rulers?

2. Describe the nature of God's laughter at wicked kings.

3. Why will wicked kings be without excuse on judgment day?

Thou Shalt Break Them

Thou shalt break them with a rod of iron;
thou shalt dash them in pieces like a potter's vessel.
—Psalm 2:9

The tenor now sings an air, a solo with orchestral accompaniment. An air, or aria, is meant to cause reflection. It is sung with emotion that touches a person's affections. Handel employs a dramatic rise and fall of notes to reflect the breaking of the wicked with a rod of iron. The music portrays a rod of iron that is lifted and brought down quickly. The intensity of the music reflects the gravity of God destroying wicked kings.

As I meditate on the seriousness of what is being said, I am reminded that God will also deal with my enemies. What a comfort to know that vengeance belongs to the Lord and I don't need to act in retaliation toward anyone.

God sovereignly controls all things in history. He has sovereign control over nations, kings, kingdoms, and every ruler. Many rulers love power and are addicted to it. They are enslaved to exercising the levers of power. Wicked rulers believe that they are in control. The kings of the earth are jealous for total control. Therefore, "the kings of the earth set themselves, and the rulers take counsel together, against the LORD and against his anointed" (Psalm 2:2).

The laws of the Communist Chinese contradict God's law. God's law says, "Thou shalt not kill." There are reports that the Chinese government forcefully harvests organs from Christians, Muslims, or other prisoners for transplant surgeries. The donors die. God's law says that His people should worship Him publicly on the Lord's Day. The Communist government forbids the worship of God in the house churches.

Our lost neighbors want to break the cords of God's control. Ordinary unregenerate Americans treat God with disdain. They want to be free to commit whatever depraved or sophisticated sin they please.

God laughs at wicked Americans: "He that sitteth in the heavens shall laugh: the LORD shall have them in derision" (Psalm 2:4). God will not be mocked. Those who challenge His rule will face swift judgment.

It is easy for God to judge His rebellious creatures. God is pictured with a rod of iron. Iron is a hard, silver-colored element. It is made up of many types of atoms that are listed in the periodic table. So God's mighty power to destroy His enemies is pictured in terms of an iron rod that He wields.

In contrast, the wicked are pictured like a piece of fragile clay pottery. Just as a dinner plate may slip out of my hands and fall on the tile floor and break in pieces, so God will easily destroy His enemies. God pictures His method of judgment as a rod of iron and the wicked like clay pottery to emphasize their fragility and His mighty power to punish them. With His iron rod He will smash them like pottery. He will end their lives in this world. And then God will punish them in everlasting hell.

Thinking It Over

1. What cords are you trying to break when you commit your pet sins?

2. In what areas do you need to repent and begin submitting to the reign of Christ?

3. How do you see God judging wicked men?

4. Is God's Word your guide, and are you seeking to obey Him out of love and gratitude? Give examples.

Hallelujah

Allelujah: for the Lord God omnipotent reigneth.
—Revelation 19:6

The kingdoms of this world are become the kingdoms of our Lord, and of his Christ; and he shall reign forever and ever.
—Revelation 11:15

KING OF KINGS, AND LORD OF LORDS.
—Revelation 19:16

Every good story has a climax, and Handel's story about the Messiah is no different. At this point all the stops are pulled. The music is robust, powerful, high, and exalting! When the English king first heard *Messiah*, he stood for this chorus. It is not clear why. In jest, some people have suggested that the king had fallen asleep and this powerful chorus surprised him and woke him up. But it is probably because Handel's stunning music combined with the marvelous biblical passages impacted the king. The "Hallelujah Chorus" led King George to rise from his seat. He wanted to show respect to the King of kings by standing in His presence.

And so it became the custom that the audience would stand when the "Hallelujah Chorus" is sung. The audience joins the chorus and soloists in showing respect to the Lord of lords. I love this tradition of standing when the "Hallelujah Chorus" is sung. I am glad that as a member of the audience I can express my devotion and reverence to the Messiah.

Are there any more majestic words of praise in any song than the lyrics of the "Hallelujah Chorus"? At this point in *Messiah*, the Christian celebrates the victory and triumph of Jesus Christ. We have followed the story of His suffering and crucifixion. We now celebrate the exaltation of the Messiah.

Hallelujah is a Hebrew word that is made up of two parts. *Hallelu* means "Praise ye," or "Let us praise." The second part, *jah*, is the covenant name of God, Yahweh. So *hallelujah* literally means "Praise Jehovah!"

To sing "Hallelujah" is an act of worship. We celebrate how Christ is worthy of being extolled, praised, celebrated, and worshiped. He is our God and Savior. We celebrate that Christ is Jehovah incarnate. Christ is our covenant-keeping God.

The psalmist exhorts, "Let every thing that hath breath praise the LORD. Praise ye the LORD" (Psalm 150:6). This last sentence reads "hallelujah" in the Hebrew. The Hebrew "hallelujah" is translated as "alleluia" in the New Testament. For example, in Revelation 19:6 the King James Version reads: "And I heard as it were the voice of a great multitude, and as the voice of many waters, and as the voice of mighty thunderings, saying Alleluia: for the Lord God omnipotent reigneth." Whether we sing in English "Alleluia" or "Hallelujah" we are expressing praise to Jehovah God.

When the great multitude in heaven cries out "Alleluia" to God, they celebrate His omnipotent power. They say: "Alleluia: for the Lord God omnipotent reigneth" (Revelation 19:6). The word *omnipotent* is found only here in the Bible, although the concept is found everywhere in Scripture. This word signifies one who possesses all power and might. When we read that God is "almighty," it is a description of an attribute that He alone possesses. There is no limit to the power of God.

In the book of Revelation, we find a celebration of the eternal reign of Christ. Heaven celebrates that "The kingdoms of this world are become the kingdoms of our Lord, and of his Christ; and he shall reign forever and ever" (Revelation 11:15). Politicians come and go. Vladimir Putin might try to reign over Russian until he is 82 years old. But not only do dictators fade away, but their kingdoms fall. Christ's dominion is forever and ever.

Thinking It Over

1. Write a prayer of praise to your covenant-keeping God.

2. Write down and memorize either Psalm 147:5 or Jeremiah 32:17 where God's omnipotence is exalted.

3. Below I recorded some famous kings or rulers from history. You have heard of many of them. Look at the length of their reign. Write a paragraph about a famous king, include the date he came to power, and how long his reign was. Compare this reign with that of the King of kings.

Kings and lords of the earth	Length of reign
King Tut, also known as Tutankhamen (of Egypt), reigned from 1332–1323 BC	10 years
Genghis Khan (of Mongolia) reigned approximately from 1185–1227 BC	42 years
Alexander the Great (of Macedonia) reigned from 336–323 BC	13 years
King Zimri (of Israel) reigned 885 BC or 876 BC	7 days
King Louis XIX (of France) reigned AD August 2, 1830	20 minutes
Henry VIII (of England) reigned from AD 1509–1547	38 years
Sobhuza (of Swaziland) reigned from AD 1899–1982	82 years

Hallelujah

Elizabeth II (of the United Kingdom)reigned from AD 1952 to present day	67 years at the present

The reign of _____ Dates of his or her reign: Extent of his or her kingdom: Interesting facts about his or her reign:	The reign of **the King of kings**

Messiah

Part 3

A Hymn of Thanksgiving for the Final
Overthrow of Death

I Know That My Redeemer Liveth

For I know that my redeemer liveth,
and that he shall stand at the latter day upon
the earth: and though after my skin worms destroy this body,
yet in my flesh shall I see God.
—Job 19:25–26

But now is Christ risen from the dead,
and become the firstfruits of them that slept.
—1 Corinthians 15:20

I am writing these words on Easter morning. The sun has risen. The birds are greeting the morning. I woke up celebrating the truth that the Messiah is risen from the dead. He is alive. And He is a sufficient and complete Savior.

The Messiah broke out of His grave around two thousand years ago. He appeared to a number of women near His tomb and surprised Mary Magdalene. As I write these words, the Messiah has taken His great power to Himself. He is exalted at the right hand of God.

The Messiah is risen. He is risen indeed!

In *Messiah*, the soloist celebrates the Easter triumph. Handel's lyricist selected two marvelous texts to sing about the resurrection of the Messiah. The first lyrics are a personal confession that Job made long ago: "For I know that my redeemer liveth, and that he shall stand at the latter day upon the earth." Job believed that his Redeemer would live! Job acknowledged the reality of his own physical death, yet he confessed the truth of his own bodily resurrection: "And though after my skin worms destroy this body, yet in my flesh shall I see God."

Job lost his material possessions, his children, and his health. He suffered excruciating pain, and his best friends tormented him. He wished that he was dead. While his body failed, he clung to the truth that his Redeemer would live. This anchored his life. Even though his life was turned upside down, he looked ahead to the resurrection of his body. And he looked forward to seeing his Redeemer.

Job had not made an idol of his possessions, his children, or his health. What about you? Are you making idols of your material possessions? Do you imagine that God owes it to you to give you continuous good health? Are you trying to cling to life in this world in perpetuity as the path to happiness? Are you frittering your life away by making an idol of yourself—seeking popularity? When you die all your bank accounts and shiny vehicles will be stripped away. God has ordained the day of your death.

Death is not pretty. By now Job's body has seen corruption. Soon after he died it was infested with worms or maggots. His body has turned back to dust. When you die your body will fall apart. Your gut is filled with bacteria, and at death they will begin to eat your body. And then there are blow flies and coffin flies that eat away at corpses.

The Messiah will give His people new bodies. Although your body is burned or is cast into the sea, the Messiah will give you a new, glorious body.

Do you have resurrection hope? Do you believe that the Redeemer lives?

The soloist not only sings out Job's confession but she also sings about how the Messiah is the firstfruits of the resurrection harvest: "But now is Christ risen from the dead, and become the firstfruits of them that slept." The apostle Paul celebrated in 1 Corinthians 15:20 that the resurrection of the Messiah is the earnest of our bodily resurrection.

Old Testament Israel celebrated the Feast of Firstfruits. God's people needed to bring the first and best of their harvest as a thank offering to God. The Feast of Firstfruits was early, at the time of the barley harvest. God's people brought the first and best of the barley harvest and waved it before the Lord. As they gave the first and best of their vegetables and fruit to the Lord, this was an earnest (a down payment) of how God would provide His people with the rest of the harvest. In the way of depending on God and thanking Him for the harvest, God would provide the complete harvest for His people.

The apostle Paul now compares the Messiah to the firstfruits that were offered to God in the Feast of Firstfruits. The harvest of the Messiah's body from the grave is the firstfruits of the resurrection harvest. The Easter triumph is evidence that God will raise our bodies from the dead on the day of the general resurrection. Just like the firstfruits were harvested first and only later would the entire harvest be taken in, so the Messiah's resurrection is historically before ours. His resurrection is also logically before ours. The reason the Messiah can raise our bodies from the dead is because He has overcome death for us.

My friend Sally lies in a rest home dying from cancer. Her body is wasting away. She cannot even get out of bed by herself, but she confesses that the Messiah is her Savior.

Spend just five minutes with young Kathleen, another resident at our local Christian rest home, and you will observe her vibrant joy. Her life has a beautiful message. Unable to control her body from falling back in her chair, she struggles to communicate with me. Her face beams and she whispers, "I am a prayer warrior." Like Job she clings to her Redeemer in hope. She has learned that Christ is sufficient.

Jesus is the first to have risen from the dead with a new glorified body. What a wonderful day it will be when the great resurrection harvest occurs! How glorious our incorruptible bodies will be!

Thinking It Over

1. What does it mean that the Messiah is our Redeemer?

2. How can you live in self-denial—-supposing that you will never die? What has helped (or can help) to cure you of this?

3. Jesus made several appearances after his resurrection! Which story excites you most? Why?

4. Why is the Messiah called the "firstfruits"?

5. What will your resurrection body be like?

Since by Man Came Death

For since by man came death,
by man came also the resurrection of the dead.
For as in Adam all die, even so in Christ shall all be made alive.
—1 Corinthians 15:21–22

In the score for "Since by Man Came Death," the musical notation *grave* is written on the top left of the page. This musical notation means that the words are to be sung in a solemn and serious way. The singer should use a restrained tone.

It is no wonder that the opening phrase "For since by man came death" should be sung solemnly and slowly. The second unhappy phrase, "For as in Adam all die," also is preceded by the notation "grave."

In the happy sections of the text, the musical notation is *allegro*. *Allegro* means that the music has a brisk tempo. That is why there is a striking contrast between the "grave" sections and the "allegro" sections. The chorus happily and briskly sings "By man came also the resurrection of the dead" and "Even so in Christ shall all be made alive."

This week I began reading through the book of Genesis. I love reading about how God spoke the word and called into being light and darkness; the firmament; the sea and dry land; the sun, moon, and stars; the water creatures and birds; all the animals and man. How beautiful God's creation was! He spoke, and it came forth. Adam and Eve were placed in the garden of Eden to dress and keep it.

God instructed Adam regarding his food: "And the Lord God commanded the man, saying, Of every tree of the garden thou mayest freely eat: but of the tree of the knowledge of good and evil, thou shalt not eat of it: for in the day that thou eatest thereof thou shalt surely die" (Genesis 2:16–17).

Adam was the first man and also the federal head of the human race. The word *federal* comes from the Latin *foedus*, which means "legal." Adam was the legal head and representative of the human race. His obedience or disobedience had implications for the human race. His sin plunged the entire human race into spiritual death: "Wherefore, as by one man sin entered into the world, and death by sin; and so death passed upon all men, for that all have sinned" (Romans 5:12). Through Adam we receive condemnation. Through Christ, elect believers receive justification.

Jesus Christ is the second Adam, and through Him we receive the free gift of justification: "As by one man sin entered the world, and death by sin; and so death passed upon all men, for that all have sinned" (Romans 5:19).

Jesus was born of the virgin Mary. The angel Gabriel told Mary that "the Holy Ghost shall come upon thee, and the power of the Highest shall overshadow thee: therefore also that holy thing which shall be born of thee shall be called the Son of God" (Luke 1:35). Jesus is the legal head of His elect, and His perfect life has implications for them. He never sinned. Jesus's righteousness is now imputed to elect believers. Even though we have not lived a perfect life, God sees us believers in Christ as having perfectly obeyed His law.

In Adam we all die. Adam experienced physical decay and finally death at age 960. His spiritual death involved him being alienated from God and placed under a sentence of the second death. But there is hope for us because just as in Adam all die, so in Christ all who believe in Him are made alive. Christ rose from the dead as the second Adam. He rose for us. Through Christ we believers will be made alive again at the last day. Our dead bodies will be raised incorruptible.

Thinking It Over

1. What do the musical notations *grave* and *allegro* mean? How does Handel use them to good effect in this song?

2. What is original guilt? How can all humans be guilty for the sin of Adam?

3. Why is the Messiah called the "second Adam"?

Behold I Tell You a Mystery

Behold, I shew you a mystery; we shall not all sleep, but we shall all be changed,
in a moment, in the twinkling of an eye, at the last trump.
—1 Corinthians 15:51–52

Agatha Christie's mysteries can keep you in suspense. Talented authors like Christie guard critical information and release it only at the right moment. A good mystery writer gives you hints, but it is only late in the book that you are able to put the clues together and figure out who did what.

Have you been in suspense about the life hereafter? The apostle Paul unveils a mystery about the sleep that is death.

Since "flesh and blood cannot inherit the kingdom of God; neither doth corruption inherit incorruption" (1 Cor. 15:50), how is it possible that we Christians will inherit the kingdom of God? Christians are flesh and blood. We have sinful and corrupt bodies. How can they be allowed into a perfect new world?

Paul does not want Christians to be ignorant and live mystified about what will happen to our bodies on the last day. Death is not the end. Paul says: "Behold, I show you a mystery; we shall not all sleep, but we shall all be changed, in a moment, in the twinkling of an eye, at the last trump."

Our corrupted and buried bodies will be changed. If a Christian lives to see the second coming of the Messiah without dying, his or her body will suddenly be changed into a new, glorious body.

While our bodies of flesh and blood can slowly fall apart, the gift of a new body will be instantaneous. How will this change take place? Will it be a slow, nine-month process? The apostle Paul is privy to this information, and he shares it with us! It will happen in a moment, as quick as a blink of an eye. As fast as the twinkle of a star, our bodies will be changed. The Messiah will recreate and perfect our bodies in the twinkling of an eye.

When will this quick change occur? Paul tells us that it will happen "at the last trump." Paul unveils the mystery in his first letter to the Thessalonians: "For the Lord himself shall descend from heaven with a shout, with the voice of the archangel, and with the trump of God: and the dead in Christ shall rise first: then we which are alive and remain shall be caught up together with them in the clouds, to meet the Lord in the air: and so shall we ever be with the Lord" (1 Thessalonians 4:16–17).

Not all people will sleep the sleep of death. At Christ's coming there still will be a few believers who are alive on the earth. God will have preserved them in the midst of the fiery persecutions of the Antichrist. Paul emphasizes that not every Christian will die; a remnant will be alive at the second coming. They will never have to die. They too will be changed—just as the bodies of their brothers and sisters who slept in Christ will be changed.

Thinking It Over

1. What is a "mystery" in the biblical sense?

2. What does Paul means when he says "we shall not all sleep"?

3. What does the Bible mean when it speaks about the saints going to "sleep" in Jesus? Does this imply the false doctrine of "soul sleep"?

4. What will you see on resurrection day?

5. What changes to your body will excite you the most at the second coming?

The Trumpet Shall Sound

For the trumpet shall sound, and the dead shall be raised incorruptible,
and we shall be changed. For this corruptible must put on incorruption,
and this mortal must put on immortality.
—1 Corinthians 15:52–53

Trumpets sound an alert. In the military, trumpets alert sleeping men that it is time to wake up: a soldier plays *reveille*.

In biblical history, trumpeters blasted on their instruments to warn a sleeping city about an imminent threat.

The Israelites heard the trumpet sound. A trumpet sounding announced that the Israelites would move camp during the wilderness wanderings. Trumpet blasts warned of a military attack. A trumpet announced the Feast of Trumpets. Trumpets announced the coronation of Solomon as king. The year of Jubilee was meant to be announced with the sound of a trumpet.

God will use a trumpet to announce the second coming of Jesus and the end of the world: "And he shall send his angels with a great sound of a trumpet, and they shall gather together his elect from the four winds, from one end of heaven to the other" (Matthew 24:31). The apostle Paul writes about the combination of the voice of a mighty archangel and the trumpet of God: "For the Lord himself shall descend from heaven with a shout, with the voice of the archangel, and with the trump of God: and the dead in Christ shall rise first" (1 Thessalonians 4:16).

Who will play the trumpet of God? Is it a mighty archangel who blows a blast on this trumpet? Will God simply cause the mighty sound of a trumpet to blast across the atmosphere?

Why will a trumpet blast fill the sky at the return of the Messiah? A trumpet blast is the sound of war. The Messiah will return to declare war upon the Antichrist and his kingdom. The trumpet blast will also be an alert so that the dead in Christ will arise from their graves. While the souls of the saints were happily in heaven, the bodies of the saints appeared to sleep in their graves. At the sound of the last trump, the bodies of the saints will awaken. Eyes will open. We will be reunited as soul and body.

The ancient custom of a year of Jubilee is a type of the marvelous freedom and celebration at the second coming of the Messiah. The year of Jubilee came once every fifty years. The year was to begin with a trumpet blast. All Jewish slaves were to be released. Anyone with debts was to be released from their obligations. If a family had lost their ancestral inheritance in the land of Canaan, the land reverted to them again. So it was a time when the poor would rejoice.

At the sound of the last trump, we will enter into our heavenly inheritance. We will enjoy the perfect freedom of the sons of God.

The apostle Paul writes that when the trump of God sounds, "the dead shall be raised incorruptible, and we shall be changed." He adds that this "mortal must put on immortality."

Paul addresses two changes that will happen to our bodies. First, this corruptible must put on incorruption. Second, this mortal must put on immortality.

Our bodies are slowly breaking down. The wise man writes poetically about these sad changes in Ecclesiastes 12:3–7:

- The keepers of the house shall tremble.
- The strong men shall bow themselves.
- The grinders will cease because they are few.
- Those who look out of the windows will be darkened.
- The doors shall be shut in the streets when the sound of the grinding is low.
- He shall rise up at the voice of the bird.
- All the daughters of music shall be brought low.

Hair turns gray, desires fail, and the body wastes away. Your molars fall out. Your hearing goes, so you can't hear your granddaughters speaking. That our bodies are corruptible means that they can fall apart. They can return back to the dust.

But this will be reversed. This corruptible must put on incorruption. In the twinkling of an eye our bodies will be so changed that they will never fall apart again. No need for knee surgery. No cancer. No aching teeth. A full head of hair.

One summer our family collected several caterpillars that were on the milkweed plants across the street. We put them in a special screen bag and added sticks and plenty of milkweed leaves for food. In a matter of days, we found caterpillars climbing the sticks and making cocoons. The cocoons hung for a few weeks until we saw gold spots appear. The cocoons took on a new look. They became a brilliant green and glowed. One morning we saw that a beautiful Monarch butterfly had emerged. The ugly caterpillar had been transformed into a fluttering orange and black butterfly. We too will be transformed!

If our corruptible is going to put on incorruption, why did Jesus's resurrection body still contain wounds? Do you remember that when Jesus appeared to doubting Thomas He said, "Reach hither thy finger, and behold my hands; and reach hither thy hand, and thrust it into my side"? (John 20:27). Why does the Messiah's resurrection body still have the marks of torture? Why is there still a wound in His side?

The Messiah left these scars in place to confirm His identity to His disciples. I am sure that the wounds did not bleed. And they were no longer painful. Perhaps the scars remain even now to remind us of the inscrutable depth of the Messiah's sacrificial love for us.

Not only must the corruptible put on incorruption, the mortal must put on immortality. That we are mortal simply means that we can die. That is why death is our last enemy. The opposite of being mortal (being in danger of dying) is to be immortal. We are mortal and die because of Adam's sin and our own sins. Genesis 2:17 informs us of the cause of death. "But of the tree of the knowledge of good and evil, thou shalt not eat of it: for in the day that thou eatest thereof thou shalt surely die." How true are the words of Isaiah 40:6–7: "All flesh is grass, and all the goodliness thereof is like the flower of the field: the grass withereth, the flower fadeth."

But on that last day we will be raised immortal! Those made from the dust of the ground will be changed. Death will be no more. Death, thou must die! You will receive a new, immortal body. You will never see death again. You will live and go on living with your resurrection body into the depths of time. We will enjoy everlasting life.

When the trumpet sounds, our bodies will be transformed. God will clothe us with incorruptible and immortal bodies.

Thinking It Over

1. Record what the following verses teach about our new bodies.

1 Corinthians 15:44	
1 Corinthians 15:49	
Philippians 3:21	

Revelation 21:4	

2. What does it mean to be corruptible? How do you see evidence of the corruptibility of your body?

3. What does it mean that your resurrection body will be incorruptible?

4. What does it mean that you are mortal?

5. What does it mean that in our resurrection bodies we will be immortal? Does this mean that we will be eternal and outside of time as God is? Will we begin to share in the divine attribute of being eternal (and be exalted above all time)?

6. What will the saints do in the world to come? What sort of gifts would you like to develop in the new world?

Then Shall Be Brought to Pass

So when this corruptible shall have put on incorruption, and this mortal shall have put on immortality, then shall be brought to pass the saying that is written, Death is swallowed up in victory.
—1 Corinthians 15:54

In this song, the saints celebrate that the day will come when "death is swallowed up in victory." What does this mean? What swallows up death? And what does it mean that death is "swallowed up in victory"?

This text is found near the end of Paul's teaching about the resurrection in 1 Corinthians 15. Paul has described two changes that Christians can expect to take place regarding their bodies:

1. The corruptible must put on incorruption.
2. The mortal must put on immortality.

Now Paul says something that the Christian can perceive is cause for celebration: "Then shall be brought to pass the saying that is written, Death is swallowed up in victory."

While passing the cemetery on my way to town I noticed workers with machinery digging a new hole. The rest of the way to town I silently contemplated death and dying. The hole they were digging was the grave for a dear member of our church who had just died after a bout with cancer.

Only a few days later, as we were celebrating a birthday with neighbors, they received word that the daughter of a close friend had just died. The young woman was only twenty-four years old.

Death is the last enemy. Death is an enemy. It is true that death is our friend because it is the means by which God brings us home. It is true that death becomes our entrance into eternal life. But it remains our last enemy. It results in separation. Yet as Christians we do not grieve as pagans. We anticipate being reunited with our loved ones who sleep in the Messiah.

What is death? Death is the end of life here on this earth. It involves a violent wrenching of soul from body. It means separation from the ones we know and love.

For those who are in Christ, death becomes a passageway into life. Our death involves also a victory as we enjoy the second resurrection—that is, the translation of our souls into the presence of the Messiah. And we will victoriously reign with the Messiah until the second coming.

God had promised in the Old Testament that death would be swallowed up in victory. That is why the apostle Paul talks about an ancient prophecy being fulfilled: "Then shall be brought to pass the saying that is written, Death is swallowed up in victory" (1 Corinthians 15:54). Already in the Old Testament the saints could hold on to this same promise. Paul quoted the prophet Isaiah, who stated, "He will swallow up death in victory; and the LORD God will wipe away tears from off all faces; and the rebuke of his people shall he take away from off all the earth: for the LORD has spoken it" (Isaiah 25:8). Jesus will abolish death!

What is swallowing what? What does it mean that "death is swallowed up in victory"? Victory is pictured as a mouth that opens up and swallows death. Just as an earthquake swallows buildings and houses, victory gulps down death. Victory is triumphant! How is it that Christ swallows down death? Already at Jesus's birth, King Herod wanted to kill Him. The people in Nazareth tried to hurl the Messiah off a cliff. The Messiah offered Himself for His people. He willingly laid down His life. He gave Himself over to death. And what do we discover on Easter Sunday? On the first day of the week the Messiah was not found in the grave because He had swallowed death by rising from the dead. That is why Jesus could tell Martha, "I am the resurrection and the life" (John 11:25).

Because Jesus has conquered death and swallowed it, we are persuaded, as was the apostle Paul, "that neither death . . . nor any other creature, shall be able to separate us from the love of God, which is in Christ Jesus our Lord" (Romans 8:38–39).

Hosea celebrated Christ swallowing up death by stating, "I will ransom them from the power of the grave; I will redeem them from death: O death, I will be thy plagues; O grave, I will be thy destruction: repentance shall be hid from mine eyes" (Hosea 13:14).\

When the last trumpet blasts, we shall be changed! Your weak body will be changed. Death will die. "And God shall wipe away all tears from their eyes; and there shall be no more death, neither sorrow, nor crying, neither shall there be any more pain: for the former things are passed away" (Revelation 21:4).

Thinking It Over

1. What is death?

2. Why do we still need to die? Didn't the Messiah die for us?

3. How does death remain the last enemy?

4. Whose death have you mourned the most? Why?

5. How have you mourned differently from atheists?

6. What does it mean that "death is swallowed up in victory"?

O Death, Where Is Thy Sting?

O death, where is thy sting? O grave, where is thy victory? The sting of death is sin; and the strength of sin is the law.
—1 Corinthians 15:55–56

The tenor and alto now sing a duet. They ask two rhetorical questions: "O death, where is thy sting?" "O grave, where is thy victory?" These are rhetorical questions, but there is an implied answer.

The answer to the question "O death, where is thy sting?" is that the stinger has been pulled out of death. As Christians, our bodies are buried in the ground like a kernel of wheat. The answer to the question "O grave, where is thy victory?" is that the grave will not be victorious over us. Christ has conquered death and the grave. Our graves will not be able to hold our bodies. Christ will burst open the tombs at His second coming.

I have lived in Southern California where there are scorpions in the deserts that sometimes wander into people's homes and sting them. The sting of a scorpion hurts. You probably would do all that you could to avoid getting stung by a scorpion. You would flail your arms to get a scorpion off your clothes. You would run from a scorpion you spotted in the carpet. You would jump out of bed if you discovered a scorpion climbing on your bed sheets. Scorpions possess a stinger on the tip of their tail. This hair-like stinger causes intense pain and swelling to the victim. The sting can be fatal.

Death is personified as a scorpion-like creature that can sting. The sting is the ability to kill a person and put him or her in the grave. This death includes both physical and spiritual death. The consequence of sin is that death can stick its fatal stinger into the fallen sons and daughters of Adam. The result is that we deserve to have our dead bodies languish in a tomb until we are raised in the resurrection to damnation (the second death).

But Christ has conquered death for His own. He has killed death. Therefore, the Messiah has pulled the stinger out of death. The Messiah said that those who believe in Him will never see death. Even physical death is only temporary. The Messiah will demonstrate the powerlessness of death when He restores our bodies to life.

When you drive past cemeteries, you might be tempted to think that the grave is victorious. The graves seem to have been able to hold their dead. I have visited cemeteries in small towns, in large cities, and in other countries. I have seen massive cemeteries in Ukraine. I have driven through large cemeteries in Grand Rapids, Michigan, and Michigan City, Indiana. Have you ever visited Arlington Cemetery near Washington, DC, to see how the graves and crosses go on and on?

So the grave might seem victorious.

But the apostle Paul celebrates that the grave will not have a final victory. Our graves will be conquered by the returning Messiah. Already now the grave has lost the victory. It is true that the grave might raise its hands in victory and tell us to take note of all the people who still lie in their tombs. But there is one who is no longer in the grave. The Messiah conquered His grave.

Therefore, the Messiah has already in principle conquered the grave. He will do this in actuality and completely at the last day.

The Messiah will soon break open your grave.

Thinking It Over

1. What is a rhetorical question?

2. What does the apostle Paul mean by the rhetorical question "O death, where is your sting?"

3. What does the apostle Paul mean by the rhetorical question "O grave, where is your victory?"

4. Where do you plan to be buried? Why?

5. Do you want your body to be buried whole? Or do you think it
    might be appropriate to have your body cremated? Why or
    why not?

6. How do you feel when you visit a cemetery?

But Thanks Be to God

But thanks be to God, which giveth us the victory through our Lord Jesus Christ.
—1 Corinthians 15:57

I'm so glad that Mr. Jennens chose the words "But thanks be to God, which giveth us the victory through our Lord Jesus Christ" as part of the libretto. Thanksgiving is a central theme in the life of a Christian. The four soloists all participate in singing this text. The soprano, alto, tenor, and bass singers echo one another as they express repeated thanks to God for giving us the victory through our Lord Jesus Christ. The singing is robust and celebrative.

In Romans 7, the apostle Paul explains the power of sin. He discusses how we, even as Christians, do things that we don't want to do. What we want to do, we don't do. What we don't want to do, we do. The good works we plan to do are left undone. Paul cries out, "O wretched man that I am! who shall deliver me from the body of this death?" In response to his own weakness and its contrast with the free grace and salvation found in the Messiah, the apostle Paul writes, "I thank God through Jesus Christ our Lord" (Romans 7:25).

We personally should express thanksgiving to God for all He has done for us. As Christians, we should say things like this:

We thank You that while we were yet enemies, You set your affection on us.

We thank You for your Son's willingness to suffer flogging and a twisted crown of thorns.
We thank You for Jesus's perfect obedience.

We thank You for our Savior's willingness to suffer nails to be to be put through His hands and feet.

We thank You for not leaving us in sin.

We thank You for Jesus!

We thank You that Jesus was willing to suffer on behalf of His people.

We thank You that Jesus was willing to leave the glories of heaven.

We thank You for Jesus's perfect holiness and purity.

We thank You for perfect salvation!

We thank You that Jesus was willing to be separated from You to pay for sin.

Thank You for demonstrating love to us.

Thank You for fulfilling everything written in the law of Moses, in the Prophets, and in the Psalms (Luke 24:44).

Thank You for being the one to redeem Israel (Luke 24:21).

Thank You that the victory is ours!

Thank You that there is salvation found in no one else but Jesus Christ.
Thank You that Jesus Christ is the Son of God!

Thank You that by believing we have life in His name (John 20:31).

Thanks be to God for completing the entire plan of salvation! How faithful our God is! Before the ages began, He planned the great work of salvation. He sent the Messiah to purchase our salvation.

We thank the Messiah for conquering death. We bend the knee to Him alone. We worship Him for His kindness and generosity.

We praise God for pouring out the Holy Spirit so that we might have a rich experience of being indwelled by the third person of the holy Trinity.

The big thing that we celebrate in this song is that God has given us the victory in Jesus Christ. This victory is comprehensive. It is a victory over death and the grave. But it is also a victory over all our enemies. It is a victory over the Devil, who will soon be under our feet. We will inherit the earth.

Thinking It Over

1. Why was the apostle Paul so thankful about when he wrote Romans 7:25

2. What are you thankful for?

3. When do you forget to be thankful?

4. What kind of triumph will you have in Jesus Christ?

5. How are you already a "conqueror," even a "super conqueror," through the Messiah?

If God Be for Us

What shall we then say to these things?
If God be for us, who can be against us?...
Who shall lay any thing to the charge of God's elect?
It is God that justifieth...Who is he that condemneth?
It is Christ that died, yea rather,that is risen again,
who is even at the right hand of God,
who also maketh intercession for us.
—Romans 8:31, 33-34

Standing on the mountaintop of faith, the apostle Paul includes two rhetorical questions. The first rhetorical question celebrates the security of the child of God: "What shall we then say to these things? If God be for us, who can be against us?" The implied answer to this question is that nothing can be against us. Paul is not so naïve to think that Christians will never face opposition. He endured fierce opposition throughout his ministry. But Paul celebrates that if God is for us (and He is), then no one can fundamentally harm us. Even our enemies are our friends! God will so override the evil actions of our enemies so that everything in our life serves our salvation. Paul had just written about something that the Roman Christians knew: "All things work together for good to them that love God." These "all things" include the attacks of enemies.

So we are secure. We are safe. If God is on our side, then He will protect us and bring us into the everlasting kingdom of His dear Son.

The second rhetorical question is, "Who shall lay any thing to the charge of God's elect?" The implied answer is that no one can. If God, the judge of all, finds a person righteous and innocent, that is the person's legal status. Why does it matter what a devil says? Why does it matter what a wicked person says about a believer? It is God who justifies. God has the authority to pardon whom He will. And no creature has a right to challenge God's legal judgment. So we are safe from any accusations of devils or reprobate people. God as judge says, "There is therefore now no condemnation to those which are in Christ Jesus, who walk not after the flesh, but after the spirit" (Romans 8:1).

The third rhetorical question is, "Who is he that condemns us?" Enemies might say that they wish we were damned to hell. They might try to condemn us to death. But what does it matter if wicked people try to condemn us if God has declared that there is now no condemnation for us? God has given to believers the right to eternal life. What does it matter if wicked people speak evil about us or try to ruin our reputations if the Messiah Himself is speaking positive words on our behalf? The apostle Paul celebrates that the Messiah makes intercession for us before the throne of God. Jesus prays for us, and His petitions are always heard.

With the Messiah on our side, we have nothing to worry about. I realize that we can get worked up about opposition. We are weak psychologically and can suffer from depression when we are attacked. But fundamentally we are safe and secure. Let wicked people attack us and speak evil about us, for we are safe in the arms of God.

That God is for us is evident from what God is doing in our lives in saving us. The apostle Paul presented what has been called the "Golden Chain of Salvation" in Romans 8:30. Salvation is pictured like a chain that is held together link by link. There are five links in this chain. God is at work in saving us; therefore, we are secure. Paul wrote about five things that God has done, is doing, or will do:

1. *God foreknew His elect.* God set His love on His elect in eternity.

2. *God predestined His elect to be changed.* God ordained that His elect would be transformed into the image of His Son.

3. *God called us.* With a sovereign effectual call, God has irresistibly drawn us to His Son in faith.

4. *God justified us.* God gave us faith in His Son and by faith alone forgave our sins, changed our legal status, and gave us the right to eternal life.

5. *God is glorifying and will perfectly glorify us.* God sanctifies us and will perfectly glorify us in the future.

God is carrying out and completing His plan of salvation.

So we are safe—now and forever. What can man do to us? What can condemn us? Next, Paul will celebrate that no one can separate us from the love of Christ. He expresses a final rhetorical question: "Who shall separate us from the love of Christ?" And the answer is that there is nothing on heaven or earth that can separate us from the love of the Messiah.

Covered by Christ's love, we have nothing to fear. God is for us!

Covered in the blood of Christ, we can say:

- God is working every detail of my life for my good.

- Those who are against me have no power over me.

- Having been made right with Christ, no one can condemn me.

- Having Christ, I have everything.

- I will not allow the approval of any human to be my idol.

- Christ is praying to the Father on my behalf.

Thinking It Over

1. What is meant by the rhetorical question "Who can be against us?"

2. Why shouldn't we be troubled by the accusations of devils or wicked people?

3. What is the answer to the rhetorical question "Who is he that condemns us?"

4. What is the answer to the rhetorical question "Who shall separate us from the love of Christ?"

5. Why are you safe (and even eternally secure) as a Christian?

Worthy Is the Lamb That Was Slain

Worthy is the Lamb that was slain to receive power, and riches, and wisdom,
and strength, and honour, and glory, and blessing. . .
Blessing, and honour, and glory, and power, be unto him that sitteth upon
the throne, and unto the Lamb for ever and ever. . . Amen.
—Revelation 5:12–14

The story of the Messiah, as told by Handel, ends with the magnificent song that the apostle John heard when he was exiled on the island of Patmos. Tens of thousands of angels announced or sang with exuberant voices, "Worthy is the Lamb that was slain to receive power, and riches, and wisdom, and strength, and honour, and glory, and blessing."

Handel uses the voices of the entire chorus to praise the Lamb who was slain. Even the four soloists participate in singing this marvelous song of praise. It is a wonder that any Christian in the audience can remain silent when they hear these words sung. What a deep impression they make.

Even though this is the last song in *Messiah*, it is the highlight. We have traced the story of the fall of Adam, the prophecies of the coming of the Messiah, His suffering and death, and His resurrection. Now the great finale is a celebration of the majesty of the ascended Messiah.

Why did the Messiah come into the world? He came to redeem a people out of all the nations of the earth who would praise and worship Him. Why is God the Father gathering a universal church out of all the nations of the world by the power of His word and Spirit? The answer: God seeks worshipers. God embarked on the great work of redemption for the praise of the glory of His grace. God seeks to extend the fame of His name. He wants to be acknowledged and celebrated for His power, righteousness, love, and grace.

The triune God embarked on the great work of redemption for the glory of the triune God. And in this song we get a glimpse of the honor that is given to the ascended Messiah.

The entire choir sings about the worth of Jesus, the Lamb of God who took away the sins of the world! He has redeemed to Himself an elect people out of the nations: "For thou wast slain, and hast redeemed us to God" (Rev. 5:9). By His obedience even to death, the Messiah has purchased a people from every country, color, race, and language for Himself. We belong to the Messiah. He makes us kings and priests. We will reign in the new world.

John saw the four beasts (glorious cherubim), the twenty-four elders (representative of the church in the Old and New Testaments), myriads of angels, and the hundreds of millions who are members of the church triumphant singing together, "Worthy is the Lamb that was slain to receive power, and riches, and wisdom, and strength, and honour, and glory, and blessing."

These verses should inspire us to worship the Lamb! We have such a small sense of the majesty of the Messiah. If we could see Jesus in His ascended glory, we would express far more praise for Him.

All of heaven celebrates the following attributes of the Messiah:

- He possesses power; He has might and dominion.

- He possesses riches; He owns the universe.

- Wisdom is ascribed to Him; He knows how best to use what He knows is true.

- Strength is ascribed to Him; He is able to defeat His enemies and carry out the sovereign will of God.

- Honor is ascribed to Him; He deserves respect and worship.

- Glory is ascribed to Him; He deserves praise.

- Finally, all blessing is ascribed to Him; He is worthy of laud.

At this point we might think every voice that might praise God has joined in this heavenly chorus. Such is not the case.

We are told that more voices join in the praise of the triune Creator: "Every creature which is in heaven, and on the earth, and under the earth, and such as are in the sea, and all that are in them" also join in praising the Lamb.

Handel uses the low voices of the tenor and bass sections of the choir to provide the effect of praise coming from deep below—from the sea and the earth. These low voices of praise provide a contrast with the heavenly voices of the sopranos. All creatures (human, angelic, and nonhuman) join together as a mighty host that praises God! All creation celebrates the Lamb. This is fitting, for all things were made by the Messiah and for the Messiah.

This praise is already now happening in heaven and earth and will go on forever and ever in the new heavens and new earth.

Long ago, King David used similar language to praise Jehovah:

> Blessed be thou, LORD God of Israel our father, forever and ever. Thine, O LORD is the greatness, and the power, and the glory, and the victory, and the majesty: for all that is in the heaven and in the earth is thine; thine is the kingdom, O LORD, and thou art exalted as head above all. Both riches and honour come of thee, and thou reignest over all; and in thine hand is power and might; and in thine hand it is to make great, and to give strength unto all. Now therefore, our God, we thank thee, and praise thy glorious name. (1 Chronicles 29:10–13)

And then *Messiah* concludes with a dramatic "amen." A huge "amen" resounds from the chorus and goes on and on. The "amens" echo back and forth. We get the idea that Handel is communicating that the Messiah is worthy of eternal praise. But the repeated "amens" are a solemn statement about the truthfulness of all that has been said and sung in *Messiah*. "Amen" is sung back and forth 138 times. Each voice among the choir and soloists agrees that the Lamb deserves all the praise.

The "amen" affirms that all that has been sung about the Messiah is true. It also means that all that has been predicted about the second coming of the Messiah is also true and will, therefore, come to pass.

Amen! *Soli Christo gloria!*

Thinking It Over

1. What creatures in heaven sing these words of praise to the Messiah?

2. What is the significance of the fact that creatures on earth join in this praise?

3. Why is it fitting that *Messiah* should conclude with these lyrics?

4. Why does *Messiah* conclude with an "amen" chorus?